NE
COMM
FO
EUR

EW
MONS
OR
OPE

Edited by Flavien Menu

Spector Books

The Un-Private Client

Architecture is a duplicitous discipline. The continual landslides between its theories, education models and effective (building) practices have rendered its original – political – focus feculent and indistinct, beyond any clear credibility.

In an era where architects could be misdoubted as the performative jesters of straightforward capitalist ruling, it is no luxury to specify (again and again) the core objective of the architectural discipline: a public profession representing not the interest of the client, but the public interest.[1]

Despite the abovementioned hymn, the 'public interest' cannot foreclose the intrinsic urge for an 'architectural client' within the contemporary architectural process. There is no such thing as architecture without clients, whether they are implicit or explicit, real or imagined, public or private, the commons, the architect-as-client...

New Commons for Europe explores the intriguingly strange interdependence between the 'architectural client' and the 'public interest', aiming to push both beyond their default *zero-sum game*[2] condition. Or how to recalibrate an architectural discipline beyond its addiction to private-gain-driven production? Fully acknowledging that by now even a 'public client' is incrementally dependent on capital appreciation and growth.

A potential way forward for a relevant and impactful architectural practice is for the architect to consequently un-privatise the 'architectural client', independent of the latter's inclination (private, public, semi-this, semi-that...). From corporate to cooperate, by which the architect will be forced to perform as a producer – not a divine creator.

The 'un-private client' could well be the missing link towards an architecture that helps to maximise and challenge 'public interest'. A non-zero-sum game.[3] The 'un-private' client as a pressing memo for architecture's endurance and sheer survival.

1 Wouter Vanstiphout, *Real Estates: Life Without Debt*, London: Bedford Press, 2014, p 62.

2 Zero-sum game: a situation in which one can win something only by causing another's loss, a gain (loss) for one must result in a loss (gain) for the other(s).

3 Non-zero-sum game: a possibility where everyone can win, a gain (loss) for one is not offset by another's loss (gain).

Towards New Commons For Europe

Change the world without taking power.
John Holloway[1]

The Bedford Tapes was held on 9 December 2016 at the Architectural Association in London. The day-long discussion brought together architects and city-makers whose actions can be characterised by the notion of 'engagement' – on personal and collective levels, questioning their ability to produce projects and spaces for the common good and its role within the civil society.

The discussion sought to support a discipline rooted in political and economic forces, using the architect's versatile knowledge to find alternative forms of profits and new types of civic spaces.

Prior to the symposium, between September and December 2016, I conducted a series of interviews throughout Europe, beginning in London and later in Berlin, Brussels, Paris, Lisbon and Bucharest. The interviews were structured around three fundamental questions, whose origins date back to an analysis of office profiles and their projects:

CONDITION

How have both global and local contexts created new forms of engagement?

ATTITUDE

What roles and tools can architects use to engage with societal agendas in their projects?

ECONOMY

What economic models can help to build socially engaged, yet sustainable and independent practices?

THE RISE OF THE COMMONS

The origins of the practices that took part in the Bedford Tapes and interviews are linked to an awareness of economic and political dysfunction and the need for fundamental and scalar changes. Indeed, many of these practices appeared following the global financial crisis of 2008. Their emergence was related to the awareness raised by the economic and political failures highlighted during the 2008 financial crisis, many were young architects – still students or sometimes already with an established office. They started seeking alternative forms of architecture practice and shared that aim while participating in the Occupy movements, engaging in local activism, and political actions that sought to create opportunities to meet and share ideals, doubts, reflections and political views.

Two main critiques emerged from the conditions during the global crisis and its impact at the local level: the role of the state in regulating its authority and the primitive accumulation of capital through individual ownership. Embedded in these are the fundamental oppositions between markets and state, public and private goods, vertical and horizontal democracy. The notion of the commons emerged as something that could offer a third way, serving as an economic platform to create values out of imperialist individual profits and as a political means for developing an alternative social contract.[2]

In economic terms, the commons highlights alternative ways of managing resources and ownership, in direct opposition to privatisation or nationalisation. Replacing rivalry of consumption with subtractability of use, the commons' economic model is based on trust, beliefs, and indulgence of groups of individuals to commonly produce and manage goods. The commons supports a network at the global level where self-organised communities are pooling resources to build social groups of responsibilities.

Based on the critique of the Hobbesian social contract, the commons embedded strong political outcomes that led the way to a new communism (common-ism)[3] where collective intelligence, communication, and exchanges produced by a community of individuals stream toward the failure of capitalism in its capacity to liberate the productive forces of individuals. Rather than forming a pyramid, as most movements do, with leaders at the top and followers below, it looks more like an elaborate web. In part, this web-like structure is inspired by the internet-based organisation. The role played by new methods of communication and the immediate worldwide connection through the use of social media has been crucial in the development of a community and the commons and has also been a powerful tool to influence decision. With the use of social media, local activism has found global echoes and a worldwide community able to offer support that was sometimes impossible to find in-situ.

PRODUCTION OF COMMONS SPACES

Shaped by broader political and economical forces, the production of space has been impacted by the rise of the commons. In Europe, the crisis acts revealed the paradigm shift within city-making and management. It came after decades of loss of public investment for culture, transportation, housing, and entire branches of public administration – resonating with the oncoming series of austerity policies.

These structural problems, which only worsened during the crisis, led to a homogenisation of urban practices and thus territories, and an increasing difficulty in producing spaces that were not commercial but 'merely' civic. The massive privatisation of public services as well as the administration and authorities in charge of city-making has led to a change in the discipline: to be able to survive in a private environment, architects have to be corporate and commercial. Regulations, insurance systems, the juridical framework imposed by private companies, bank and investment funds in charge of funding urban development only allow the choice to be corporate or to die.

In 'Reclaiming the Commons' by Naomi Klein,[4] the term 'commons' applies to the urban-encompassed non-appropriable space, beyond the public and the private, a resource for collective life. The growing privatisation of urban spaces, and more broadly the privatisation of all aspects of everyday life and the transformation of all activities into commodities, furthered the need for architects to take new, socially-motivated measures.

Sharing this view and finding alternative ways, a shared desire to find new commons that escaped privatisation but does not rely too heavily on state support emerged. In Paris, Berlin, Brussels, London, Lisbon, Bucharest, and many other European cities, the need to find alternative resources for producing new types of public goods forced individual young architects to group into collectives and take responsibility for creating changes and taking action within civil society.

The wide reach of the concept of the commons[5] resonates with an architecture that goes beyond the boundaries of its discipline, using the architect's tools to engage with surrounding problems. The commons is a space between the public and the private, in the urban realm or in its financing: architecture refuses to be a product or a service and seizes on collective necessities. The production of the commons, spatially, presents a new notion of sharing, negotiation, and usage; architecture seeks to create new political forces, new ways of acting, and new forms of the local. These new architectural practices were spurred by the urgent need to act – to battle for non-market spaces, for shared civic spaces. Above all, these spaces are defined by their use and not by their property; they are spaces governed by participatory processes, inviting processes that allow for shifting programmes and open uses.

POOLING THE COMMONS

This book is a transmission of the thoughts and reflections that animate these collectives. It is seizing a moment. It offers a snapshot of an emerging generation of architects – one that appeared spontaneously and simultaneously on European grounds – committed to the development of collective social agendas and practices.

Interviews and discussion are merged into a stream of texts that follows the natural path of a day of conversation. The live material brought together various subjects that cross discussion between invited practices and presented projects. Crisis suddenly revealed how much architecture is at the mercy of broader economic and political forces: massive migration of labour, austerity measures, lack of public funding. This reality compelled architects and students to get out of their comfortable echo chambers and to break the protective wall of cultural self-indulgence. Faced with these findings, resistance has developed towards a form of practice independent of the traditional paths of the profession. Leave school before graduating. Do not wait for a client but provoke it. Do not respond to a programme but create it. Consider no longer the architect as a producer of services or architecture as a product. These alternative attitudes reflect a desire for immediacy, an urge to 'transform the act of building into a political act',[6] as Anthony Engi Meacock of Assemble says in his interview. The operating methods of such ambitions require an increased attention to local needs; a thorough knowledge of the urban, legal, or financial context; but also, and above all, spontaneity and naivety. The project as such is written collectively – not just between experts – and convenes civil society.

Making a project becomes the making of society. An empty parking lot starts hosting a public house with free water (raumlabor), a former military compound becomes a testing ground for local democracy (ateliergeorges), an illegal collective kitchen is created in the outskirts of a refugee camp (Ateliermob). Often temporary, these projects emphasise collective design and construction processes rather than ex-post use.

The emergence of the commons underpinned the emergence of alternative values. But today, the economic vulnerability of these collectives demands new economic models: raising public and private funds, calls for individual contributions, corporate social responsibility – like subsidies. They also need the use of new tools to advocate their position, enabling them to find legitimacy to achieve self-financing: Assemble lectures on their ultra-local project around the world; Ateliermob influences political decisions in Latin America through its Twitter account; Jack Self crowdfunds to publish books.

As Markus Bader of raumlabor points out, 'in a situation where resources are scarce, the most important thing is to know where to place added value'.[7] The emergence of these practices tests how to create alternative forms of projects – new spaces between private and public, between commercial and residential; interstitial spaces often denied but which can become formidable engines of non-commercial spaces. To quote the former director of the Tate Modern, Chris Dercon, 'We need to create spaces that give us confidence to invent new public forms'.[8]

1 John Holloway, *Change the World Without Taking Power*, London: Pluto Press, 2003.

2 Elinor Ostrom, *Governing the Commons*, Cambridge: Cambridge University Press, 2015; and Ostrom Elinor, Nobel prize lecture, 2009.

3 Alain Badiou & Slavoj Žižek, *L'idée du Communisme: Conférence de Londres*, Fécamp: Editions Lignes, 2009.

4 Naomi Klein, 'Reclaiming the Commons' in *New Left Review* 9, London: New Left Review, 2001, pp 9–81.

5 Michael Hardt & Antonio Negri, *Commonwealth*, Harvard: Harvard University Press, 2009.

6 Interview with Anthony Engi Meacock, 5 October 2016, London.

7 Interview with Markus Bader, 13 October 2016, Berlin.

8 Interview with Chris Dercon, 23 February 2016, London.

Holly Lewis, We Made That

Blackhorse Lane, London

Holly Lewis, We Made That I'm going to present our project in Blackhorse Lane, in Walthamstow. This was a project for Waltham Forest Council. The area features a large plot of industrial land right next to quite a large residential area, right next to an enormous area of marshes and wetlands. It's also a huge growth area for the Borough of Waltham Forest. And obviously in London you try to build houses – as many as you can, wherever you can. The borough is looking at this area as a place to build houses, although traditionally it has been industrial.

There are all kinds of interesting things that have been made there and are still made there including wooden pipes and chocolate puddings. But because the borough is looking at the area as a site to build new houses, it's facing a lot of change in its future; and across London there is a threat that industrial land – and we know this from some other research that we have done – might disappear quickly due to housing pressure. And once you turn industrial land into housing, it's really unlikely to return to the earlier economic activities there. The demand for housing is too high. And although Blackhorse Lane is its own place and it has its own character, it is also quite typical compared to other places in London. It has some characteristics that are common to other places of regeneration and growth, which are really interesting to us. So our response is both to this place and also to how we can approach other places like it in London.

Our work was funded by the Mayor's office and the idea was to look at this high street. The funding that they had was meant to support high streets but in this case the high street had a number of components. Indeed, it is a high street that crosses a variety of neighbourhoods. So at the extreme south you have a collection of little shops, the northern part is this industrial area, and past the industrial area is the existing residential neighbourhood. We are trying to kind of grapple with all these different parts of what's happening in the area.

The brief was to help the high street perform better and that meant aesthetic changes but also ways of integrating the industrial areas with the high street – to give them a better face. Our actions were trying to change the perception of the industrial boxes from the residents' point of view. We tried to help them change the way they look at the industrial land, not only thinking about it as big sheds with weird and dirty things inside but as something good for the economy and the vibrancy of the area. Essentially, through a regeneration project, we tried to celebrate everyday uses, from retail to light industry, because this is part of the city's diversity.

Our proposals were focused on the entrances to the industrial estate and on the little run of shops. The brief was to focus on the frontages of those estates, the public realm in front of them and the shop fronts. The brief was subject to a little bit of wilful misinterpretation by us – we interpreted it a bit more broadly.

BLACKHORSE PROPERTIES
PROPERTIES
CAFE
Est. 1925
RODI
Krishna News
KRISHNA NEWS
BH
BUS STOP
Forest Road
towards
St James Street
158
CHAUDHRY
FOOD & WINE
DRY CLEANERS
BLACKHORSE ROAD STATION
YOUR LOCAL NO.1
ESTATE AGENT

There were some functional issues that we found – people found it really difficult to navigate around there. They didn't know where they were going. If you were trying to get to the industrial estate there was no particular way of knowing that it was *that* entrance and not one of the other four or five entrances nearby, which created challenges for vehicles and for people navigating the area. It was also all looking a bit shady and not necessarily communicating its value; that may sound superficial but it's very important.

We made some fairly straightforward design responses: improvements to the pedestrian environment, to the footways and the public realm; some slightly more quirky things: a facelift to a food store, which gives the owner a lot more confidence with a very small budget. We also delivered a sign to the owner, which says the name of his business, Grab and Go. The sign spins in the wind, which I think was a surprise to our client – I don't think he understood that from the drawing.

This was an incremental aggregated approach to delivering projects in the public realm. In previous lectures when I have shown this project I have described it as a 'marginal gains' approach. The idea is that you do things on a small scale and put them together rather than produce one shiny thing at one end of the road.

We worked with the graphic designers Europa and the businesses' owners to create new way-finding signage that lists all the businesses and locates visitors in relation to those places and to put together a directory of everything that's happening in the area. We ended up with rich – we think quite exciting – streetscapes that assemble elements that can seem a bit surprising, but also serve a functional purpose. Like the clock we designed on Blackhorse Lane, which says, 'This is a place with a character we can be proud of'. It has been adopted as a bit of a – I don't want to say icon – as something that people are aware of. We've heard that new businesses give their location in relation to the clock.

We also looked at the little run of shops, which are significant because they are on the route between the tube station and the rest of the industrial area. We used the same robust typography and colours that are used in the industrial area to refresh these shops. We were able to work with every single one of the businesses. We tried to find some aesthetic commonality between the two areas, but also to just acknowledge that these businesses are great and to encourage the new residents to not dismiss some of the smaller businesses.

Our interventions were mostly physical but we took a slightly broader interpretation of the brief and we were really keen to celebrate what was happening inside some of the big industrial sheds in the area. We worked with the photographer Thomas Adank who went to some of the businesses and took

GO

portraits of what was happening, and we put those photos onto billboards. Through working with Thomas and his particular aesthetic eye, we sought to ask people to look with fresh eyes at the area.

We also ran a sign-making workshop in Blackhorse Workshop, which is an Assemble project. The idea was that Blackhorse Workshop just opened (it was part of the same funding programme to support the economy of the area) and they were trying to bring together makers from the area. The sign-making was related with the shopfront programme that we were running, so we were trying to bring people together with this programme of activities. There are some things that we can't take any credit for but Blackhorse Workshop has continued to offer this type of training and skills programme.

After we finished the project, we began working with the Waltham Forest Council to put together a funding bid for a housing zone in the area. They now have funding through the Mayor's office; I think it's 30 million pounds for delivering 1,500 new homes but also 1,000 new jobs. We also worked with them to develop a series of proposals, which we titled a 'Creative Enterprise Zone'. These are economic initiatives that try to support creative businesses to come and locate in the area, which was where it got really exciting for us. For us, it's not just about making nice looking things, but it is about developing the character of the area – where the jobs are, who's working there – and about balancing growth with employment, which is something that is slightly more forward-thinking than the typical attitude across London to these industrial places.

My partner and I were there yesterday and it seems to be actually working. There are new businesses: a business called Blackhorse Lane Ateliers is making jeans in the area and references the clock on their website. There is also an antique scooter place that has now relocated to Blackhorse Lane and they are all using the aesthetic of the wayfinding and there seems to be a pride and interest in relocating to this area.

Again, I don't think that we can take all the credit, but I think by titling and giving validity to this place as having its own character, which it never previously would have had or felt – it was just a tube stop in many people's minds – contributes to thinking slightly more broadly about how regeneration can play out in some of these challenging edges of London.

Flavien Menu Blackhorse Lane is a really interesting and attractive area now; it's on the Victoria Line, close to the city centre. It is true that it has been depreciating in the last decades but now there is a rising appetite for building in the area. Your project, as well as Blackhorse Workshop by Assemble, is making the area visible and attractive. There is a rising tension between the

B L A C K H O R S E LA NE

need for housing and the creative industry that gives a sense of place to this area. Massive property developments are arriving; it's happened next to Blackhorse Workshop. In front of the workshop, which was a former tyre replacement garage, there are now more than 100 homes under construction. It seems to be a classic case of gentrification: some creative pioneers not afraid of the roughness of the area came, gave value to the land, and then property developers came to harvest the grapes of years of urban activation. How can you tackle this? How is your initiative not only a transitory project but one that can also help to keep industry within the city?

Holly Lewis Our project tries to work with economic growth, augmenting and shaping the creative enterprise initiatives that are real. There's money behind them. I can imagine a parallel world where none of these projects happen, and none of the money that came from the GLA, the Greater London Authority, and spent by Waltham Forest Council was spent. And that's what you get with the generic houses built with no thought about how to integrate with the area or what the economy of that place might be in the future.

We did things on billboards. Big signs might seem superficial but we can't always be humble and say, 'We have to be quiet and meek and sensitive'. We have to state the importance of our work and collaborations really loudly in order for people to understand that these are great things.

We are trying to balance basic things about how people live in the city with some bigger ideas about place and economy. It is a charm offensive but it is genuine. Spending 13 million pounds in one way instead of 13 million pounds in a different way is significant to me. What it seeks to do is make these housing developments that you can dismiss for being generic into something appealing – to make sure that people that want to come and live in those places and can look across the road and instead of thinking, 'Oh, that's shit' they can say, 'Oh, interesting. Maybe I want to work there, maybe somebody else works there'.

When we started working on it, you probably wouldn't have heard of Blackhorse Lane and now it feels like there is something happening there. And whether that's just gentrification or whether it has some components that are more valuable, it is a conversation that would be interesting to have. I think it is better to try and do these kinds of things than to not bother.

Joachim Declerck You are presenting the project as if everybody was convinced of it; you didn't tell us what the resistance was. Who did you have to convince and how did they get convinced that you should not explore how this could be a zone for maximising housing in terms of volume, in terms of quantity? You

Stations (North – South)	% of workforce in Creative Industries	Largest Creative Sub-Sector	% of workforce in largest sub-sector
Walthamstow Central	4.4%	IT, Software & Computer Services	1.2%
Blackhorse Lane	**12.5%**	**Creative Manufacturing**	**8.5%**
Tottenham Hale	4.0%	Creative Manufacturing	2.2%
Seven Sisters	6.0%	Creative Manufacturing	4.1%
Finsbury Park	5.0%	Film, TV, Video & Radio	1.0%
Highbury & Islington	8.5%	Music, Performing & Visual Arts	1.8%
King's Cross St Pancras	11.9%	Publishing	3.2%
Euston	10.6%	Museums, Galleries & Libraries	5.3%
Warren Street	19.8%	Advertising & Marketing	7.8%
Oxford Street	25.2%	Film, TV, Video & Radio	10.7%
Green Park	12.4%	IT, Software & Computer Services	3.8%
Victoria	8.6%	Advertising & Marketing	2.6%
Pimlico	2.8%	IT, Software & Computer Services	0.9%
Vauxhall	9.1%	IT, Software & Computer Services	4.8%
Stockwell	3.8%	IT, Software & Computer Services	1.2%
Brixton	4.8%	Film, TV, Video & Radio	1.8%
London	*9.7%*	*IT, Software & Computer Services*	*2.5%*

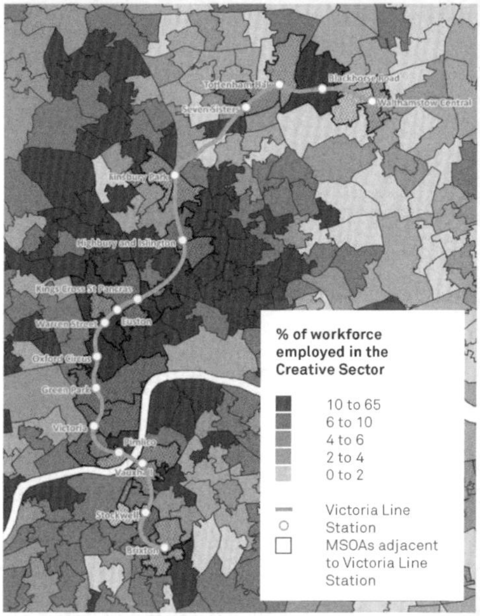

Source: Regeneris Consulting & BRES (2013)

are presenting it as if everybody was already convinced that it should be strengthened as a special economic urban environment. How did you build your argument to convince the others?

Holly Lewis There was a sequence of decisions that were made, and some of those decisions had already been made by the time we became involved. The decision to release some of the industrial land had been protected by policy, and the decision to turn land into housing had already been made. The decision to spend money on trying to improve the entrances to the industrial area had already been made. The idea of the Creative Enterprise Zone came from us pushing for it. And that gave specificity and character to an idea that they already had. If you talk to regeneration people, you talk in numbers of houses or jobs. And what we did was try to give some character to that, and try to talk about how industrial and manufacturing activities are part of the DNA of the area. But it wasn't like we were in charge of the conversation.

Joachim Declerck What I am actually trying to find out is if you have the feeling as an office that you're involved in setting the tone of the debate in a city and environment like London. Saying there is something that is important, shouting it out loud. And this generates, by coincidence, this project, but it could have been another one or maybe it's three in a row on this subject. Is this attitude toward brief and project a guideline in your practice?

Holly Lewis Yes. We were doing this project and that turned into us working on a London-wide study of industrial land, in parallel with AECOM. The ability to do that is really interesting; that's now shaping some of the conversations that are being had. There was an agenda within the GLA, which is why they commissioned a report, but some of that is now feeding what the new mayor is saying.

In projects like this, we say, 'This is strategic, this is a masterplan'. We think of all these little signs and the café and the shops and workshops as a masterplan. Increasingly we are now being commissioned for projects that are more involved in strategic decisions. For example in Kingston, the plan drawn for Crossrail 2 put nine new stations in the borough, which would introduce a massive change in the borough. You can now build tons of new housing around there. And in those conversations we were able to say, 'This piece of industrial land should be protected'. We are generally advocating for housing or jobs. We are really interested in getting ourselves into positions of more strategic decision making. Getting further upstream in the decision making of an architectural project is part of our office strategic position. We have to have the research and the

Our project tries to work with economic growth, augmenting and shaping the creative enterprise initiatives that are real.

We are trying to balance basic things about how people live in the city with some bigger ideas about place and economy. It is a charm offensive but it is genuine. Spending 13 million pounds in one way instead of 13 million pounds in a different way is significant to me.

masterplanning and the delivery projects – the interrelationships between all of those is capital for being able to infiuence the project from its beginning. If we were just at the delivery end of things, we'd be missing a lot of tricks that we don't want to miss.

Joachim Declerck One last question: how do you sustain this advocating for certain things, researching pieces, doing projects? Is that a piece of work in the office? You list the three types of work but you didn't list how you curate the coherence between them, how you finance them, how you make it all work.

Holly Lewis They are all bits of work that are commissioned by the public sector. Sometimes we partner with economists, like in the case of the Creative Enterprise Zone. All of the delivery projects are commissioned and the strategic work is commissioned. So we find a thread between all of the parts, which for us is just common sense. That is, when you're delivering something you're also thinking about what's happening there: we see very clearly the link between the economic character of the place and the physical character of the place. For instance, everyone was surprised that we partnered with economic consultants – for us it makes total sense to do that.

Harriet Harriss I want to return to the conversation about gentrification. I suppose some people might consider your work as contributing to gentrification but you're raising some interesting questions about the display of culture and the aesthetics of cultural production, not just consumption. Design is often considered to be an economic activator but this is largely credited to starchitects' bold schemes, which instead just use design to generate profits for investors and create exclusive, elite spaces.

In contrast, what you're doing is leveraging value within this particular community. It's also interesting to view your work in a globalised context: only 10 per cent of the UK's GDP is manufacturing-derived, so you're dealing with something that is a scarce resource and leaves us vulnerable in terms of global trade and economic sustainability. Your comment about shouting about the importance of the project and the capacity of architects to initiate projects that expand into other ventures is a brilliant illustration of the activator potential of grassroots design.

Holly Lewis We've been working on industrial areas' urban issue in a number of different places in London. Even within those places manufacturing is a small component – transport and logistics are much more prominent. What the

Getting further upstream in the decision making of an architectural project is part of our office strategic position. We have to have the research and the masterplanning and the delivery projects – the interrelationships between all of those is capital for being able to influence the project from its beginning.

London-wide industrial land study showed is that the land has been lost at a much greater rate than was anticipated; we eventually get to the point where what's left is less than what we need. So when you say 10 per cent of the GDP is in manufacturing it sounds small but there's all this other kind of richness. It can be characterised as being a small part but actually there is all this other stuff that happens in those places. They're vital to the city.

Joachim Declerck In Belgium, 80 per cent of the companies are in urban environments. They produce 50 per cent of the GDP. It is not just manufacturing, but also logistics, recycling – everything is there. This holistic view is much more important than everything we learn through looking only at statistics and only at hand labour or manufacturing. So there is really an argument to be built – that's what you're doing – for the fact that we need to mix much more and capture the dynamics of a growing city to produce new spaces for these types of activities. In that sense there really is a project.

Holly Lewis And that's a design challenge. That's where you need an architect who's doing great things.

Pooja Agrawal Industrial land, and the impact of the loss of industrial land to London's economy, is a theme that has been of keen interest to the GLA, especially in the last ten years. We have mapped areas such as Park Royal in great detail, and this evidence has enabled us to protect existing industrial land in the emerging draft of the new London Plan. Spatially, architects now have an exciting role to look at how different typologies of uses can work well together, in the scale of neighbourhoods such as Blackhorse Lane, to the scale of a building where interesting typologies are emerging in areas such as Hackney Wick.

I think what's really remarkable about We Made That is how successful you are as a business. But in a time of austerity, where across London we are seeing authorities' regeneration teams disappearing, how sustainable is it for you to rely on the public sector for work in the next ten years?

Holly Lewis We work in the public sector not because we think it is the way to make the most money. We work in the public sector because that's what we are interested in doing; choosing taps for rich people is not something that I care to do. But actually, the reality that we have seen – and it's a cynical, horrible, factual one – is that local authorities are looking for other people to deliver the things that they still have to do.

We work in the public sector not because we think it is the way to make the most money.

The reality that we have seen – and it's a cynical, horrible, factual one – is that local authorities are looking for other people to deliver the things that they still have to do.

Our growth is probably in a nasty way related to the retraction of the public sector.

We are able to do that, and I hope that we do it with a kind of a good heart and ethic. Our growth is probably in a nasty way related to the retraction of the public sector. We always think that in the past – a few decades ago – we probably would have been working in the public sector but that isn't an opportunity that is available to us, so we're doing it this way.

The regeneration teams are diminishing and we are delivering some of those services that still have to be delivered, particularly in London. London's still growing, so somebody is either shaping how it grows or spending the planning gain that is received from that growth. We are involved in that conversation so we are much more tied to growth more generally than we are tied to what the public sector is directly delivering. So it doesn't seem to be a threat so far, but it might just all die and then we are in trouble. (*Laughs.*) But so far it works and the public sector still spends a lot of money. It is spending less money but there is a lot of stuff that happens and that has to keep happening.

Pooja Agrawal If a private developer whose past work you do not ethically agree with, comes to you asking you to deliver a really interesting typology, looking at manufacturing and residential, would you say no?

Holly Lewis We would say no.

Jack Self I think it is really interesting that you present this project. I know the project reasonably well but have not seen it presented. One of the things that I've thought about this project – which I was waiting for you to say – is that, without overly theorising it, Marx says that in order for class struggle to exist, the classes have to already find a way to represent themselves. Aesthetics and representation become extremely important and in that sense mass communication shapes how you think about graphic design and street presentation. We talk about community building often in a superficial, meaningless way. You've taken a row of shops that have no obvious connection and you've applied something as simple as a uniform typeface and colour palette. Suddenly what you create is not just an actual connection between them in terms of a common project, but also it's impossible for someone to go in and pick them off one by one, because they are part of a consistent whole. The symbolism of that aesthetic is super important for protecting these types of zones. Do you have something to say about that?

Holly Lewis I could never say that myself because that would be so egocentric but it's nice that you say it. (*Laughs.*) I sort of agree with you. I wouldn't want

Marx says that in order for class struggle to exist, the classes have to already find a way to represent themselves. Aesthetics and representation become extremely important and in that sense mass communication shapes how you think about graphic design and street presentation.

to overstate the unity between those shop owners though. I think Pooja could agree with me. (*Laughs.*)

Melanie Dodd I would like to go back to what you said about 'rewriting the brief'. Twenty years ago, I recollect using this term – understanding that rewriting the brief was very much about 'resisting' the normative constraints of a given brief/client. Public realm projects by architects were almost non-existent at that time – except for the Bankside Redevelopment 'Future Southwark' pioneered by Southwark's Director of Regeneration, Fred Manson. I wondered to what extent you feel that the brief now needs less rewriting because authorities are somehow more enlightened?

Or do you still think that there is still a role for resisting those macro policies – policies that could be a bit diluted when they come to the level of delivering?

Holly Lewis I think it varies widely depending on what you're talking about. We recently worked in a borough on the farthest edge of London. That was challenging. They were much more comfortable in their brief and found it challenging when we tried to expand it. Yes, we are massively entitled to that sort of approach of practice.

Peter Swinnen On the one hand I congratulate you with this project; I think it's a very ethical project – in the most sincere way – at the same time I find it an extreme pity when I hear you say you only wish to work for the public sector. In a time where the public sector is abdicating, this statement seems impotent. Your kind of approach, your sensitivity, and your sense of complexity are also needed in the private sector. Maybe not today, but in a couple of weeks' or months' or years' time you might reconsider saying no to the private sector, because the private sector is in deep need of this kind of attitude and intelligence. I don't think it's either/or; in a way there's no choice. I think the public sector doesn't exist anymore; there is something else happening: a grey zone between private interest and public good that needs to be activated with intelligence and ethics.

Holly Lewis I am being slightly simplistic in saying no to this question 'would you deliver an interesting typology for a private developer?' We struggle.

Peter Swinnen Imagine if delivering such interesting typology would be the stepping-stone for you to get a foot in the door and then to actually be able to infiltrate this realm. I believe such shift is extremely crucial.

I find it an extreme pity when I hear you say you only wish to work for the public sector. In a time where the public sector is abdicating, this statement seems impotent.

Your approach, your sensitivity, and your sense of complexity are also needed in the private sector.

The private sector is in deep need of this kind of attitude and intelligence.

Holly Lewis Whenever we talk about the private sector we say all our work is public, we don't say all of our work is for the public sector. That is the thing that underpins it and recently we have been doing a little bit of work for a developer because the borough in this particular instance is going into a joint venture with the developer. But we've also been approached by developers – really horrible approaches. They just assume that we will drop everything and put all our resources into their projects. And we say, 'If there's a public ambition for your projects, then yeah, sure'. But we don't see that actually. We're open to working with developers who have a commitment to what we can do for a certain place. If we found one, we would do it. But we don't.

The public sector doesn’t exist anymore; there is something else happening: a grey zone between private interest and public good that needs to be activated with intelligence and ethics.

Aurélien Delchet & Mathieu Delorme, ateliergeorges

Caserne Melinet, Nantes

Aurélien Delchet, ateliergeorges Caserne Melinet is an urban redevelopment project in Nantes. Nantes is one of the most dynamic cities of France. They build around 600 homes a year, which is a lot, and Nantes is still a small city. There is a derelict, 14-hectare military base where a public planner is building 1,700 homes. It is one of the most important projects for the city at the moment. We are working on the urban design as part of a larger team of designers, but we are identified as the landscape architects and the ones managing the public consultation.

The site is located a five-minute walk from the train station, which means that it is surrounded by historic urban fabric – mainly small detached houses with gardens. The mayor of Nantes is leading the project. It was a classical project brief: masterplanning with a public participatory process, then new construction. However, because of the specificity of the neighbourhood, which has small houses with small gardens, it was not interesting for us to go into a traditional participatory process. Instead, we were interested in trying to make connections and developing relationships within this NIMBY context, whose close residents had serious concerns about the 1,700 new homes, including a large amount of social housing. So we tried to develop a 'project community' to get people involved in the project development process. We opened the door to them, we gave them the right to speak and come along with us to build the project together.

The main stake for us here was the inventive economy. When we learned that 70 per cent of the buildings were going to be demolished, we wondered how to use the rubble from the demolition – which was not part of the initial contract. We had to negotiate with the city and bring along an association of architects called Bellastock, who are experts in demolishing and reusing building materials.

The demolition is now ongoing. Georges and Bellastock worked with a demolition company to invent processes of careful disassembly. We needed to be able to reuse the bricks, so we couldn't just knock down the buildings without a strategy. The demolition process was very experimental; we tried some things that didn't work, and some worked perfectly. In the masterplan there was a park planned at the north end of the site. This is where we decided to store the gained materials. Most of this resource will be reused to build urban furniture.

In parallel, during a public consultation session we proposed to make a participatory building site with the people from the neighbourhood. People were eager to be involved deeper in a project that was not planned, that was not part of our initial mission. We negotiated with the city to make it possible. We held workshops over the course of a few weekends to work on the specified area around the 'project house' where we exhibited the evolution of the project

OCCAMAT

and informed people about the project. We also built a few benches with some locals – we used the wood from the carpentry and the stones from existing buildings and it ended up being a bench. We set up the public realm like a small square. We were trying to experiment and push things forward, to work on the 'project house' and its surrounding public realm. We were trying to co-create or co-rebuild it with locals who were involved in the project.

Mathieu Delorme, ateliergeorges We also want to present something related to the project that covers the broader scope of our thinking. We are developing two books: the first on urban economy and the second on urban ecology with the economist Isabelle Baraud-Serfaty and the architect Mathias Rollot. These two books relate to what we always try to develop within our projects: economy and ecology. We like to act when the project becomes a process and when the designer becomes a strategist. By 'ecology of the project' we mean that we foster collective intelligence – we ask, 'where should we act?' or 'how should we act?' – it could be around natural resources, public realm, building or a building typology. And by 'economy of the project', we mean that we are focused on producing an inventive combination of operational tools that look at the way we fabricate or build the city.

In the first book – an illustrated manual of basic urban economy tools – we are trying to express, in simple terms, how buildings and cities are made economically. A lot of students in architecture schools don't know about the economic ecosystems of city making. And many architects are unable to disrupt economic ecosystems, so we are trying to explore some simple hypotheses on how to make affordable housing without public support, for example. Using simple drawings, we try to explain how the city is built and to express the role and the importance of stakeholders, investors and banks. We also explain the complexity of the land – intervening in de-industrialised areas versus the city centre demands for different understandings of economy.

The second book is more about the ecology and the ecosystems of competencies that can be activated during a project. It looks at how we can find new approaches to process with every project. In Nantes, we worked with Bellastock but for another project we worked with Yes We Camp, a French architecture association. We have met with almost twenty architecture collectives in France in order to know what they can do, what they want to do, and how we can involve them in public consultations. We've mapped different collectives and we try to dig into their main expertise and protocols.

These two books react to the actual economical context that we face. In France it's really complicated: the most ambitious projects are sustained with a lot of public money. But public money is less and less available, so we are also

attempting to work with developers in virtuous ways. As urban planners, we are really linked to the public sector. While we know how to engage with it in a traditional way, we also want to improve it collectively and make some changes because we think the model is in need of reform. And it is complicated! Sometimes just filling out the administrative forms is so complicated that we almost miss out on the project itself because of the weight of bureaucracy.

In Nantes, we had to convince the public administration to allow Bellastock to work with us and to develop a little administrative strategy to make it happen. We try to make the link between alternative ethical urban approaches and the classic bureaucracy characterising the public sector and the French way of making cities.

We don't simply call other architecture collectives when the project funds are low and we need people working for little money. We call them for their own vision and their own way of doing things. In the end, it's not so cheap, because we try to make sure they have their own sustainable economic model. Sometimes it is complicated as they are experiencing economic pressure, asking whether they can earn money in these collaborations. We try to explain that you can earn enough money to live, involved in such urban projects. We need to reinvent the way to find financial support and involvement. Nantes is a testing-ground to experiment with a new economic lever, because the classic urban economic model is not working anymore anywhere.

Jack Self You began by talking about the people of Nantes and their gardens. Protecting one's garden, in the classic Voltairean sense, seems to be a good place to start to think about what it means for 2016. Beginning with David Cameron and ending with Matteo Renzi, we have seen politicians make one fatal fiaw: they ask the population to vote on their leadership; and there is probably no government in the world, certainly in Europe, that the people would say, 'Yeah we think you're great'.

People are generally unhappy about many things. One of the consequences is a huge amount of nostalgia and a huge amount of desire for things to stay the same. What I want to know more about is how you worked with the local people to create a positive vision. Often during the consultation process you get a group of people whose starting position is, 'We shouldn't even be in this meeting because they should never have imagined doing 100, 1,000 homes in the first place'. I am interested in how you moved from that to such a positive discussion.

Mathieu Delorme Our first meeting with locals was in a room filled with 300 people. They came because they literally wanted to argue. We carefully explained

our method. Yes, we were in charge of the design and urban planning, but we also insisted on our desire to build the project together. There is no mediation between the panel and the team. We are in direct link and totally transparent. We have shown them the schedule and we said, 'Okay, we will meet every month for a year'. We stuck to this commitment. One Saturday morning per month we met with the local people – eighty of them. It was a really long process that created strong involvement in the project. In the first six months we tried to get to know each other. Six months later we did a general public presentation of the project. We fiipped the roles and asked people to present the project with us. It created a completely different atmosphere.

We created an atmosphere of mutual trust and we also tried to make people understand the complexity of developing such a project. We discussed different topics linked to the project and tried to find collective solutions. We worked through scenarios and it was not easy – either for us or for them – but it allowed people to understand that solutions are not one-sided, especially when building an entire area of a city!

We signed a six-month contract that has been extended for nearly 18 months in total. The good thing is that the locals want to create an association and to run the project house: turning the derelict building into a place with a mixed programme including a bar, a café, a restaurant, a fab lab, etc. The new association that will take care of the 'project house' will receive public funds for helping to run its activities.

Flavien Menu For the past decade, participation in planning and design has been a big trend across Europe – and there are a lot of redundant questions about who's participating and what kinds of things they want to protect. Often the people who participate are mainly there to protect self-interest and individual privileges. So how do you keep the project in line with your first intention and how do you resist the NIMBY attacks? How do you keep your ideals without being too disrupted by collaboration, participation, and related consensual attitudes?

Mathieu Delorme We are not asking them the big questions. We discuss only specific topics. We were selected by the city for our project and we are defending our project. So we are not compromising the big picture but only sharing questions linked to the main ambition. We explained to the people that we were chosen by the politicians that they elected. It is also our role to be pedagogic about the democratic system of city-making and we explained to them that they are part of it, that they are participating in determining the answers to specific

One Saturday morning per month we met with the local people. It was a really long process that created strong involvement in the project. In the first six months we tried to get to know each other. Six months later we did a general public presentation of the project. We flipped the roles and asked people to present the project with us. It created a completely different atmosphere.

questions. Citizens have to acknowledge that they gave power to certain elected bodies to make decisions for them about broader policies and the built environment.

Jack Self I think that's such an important point. At the moment there is so much discussion about the structure of democracy itself and one of the things I find very troubling is that there are not questions about whether one party or another party wins, but a lot of questions about if democracy is the right structure for society, which, frankly, terrifies me. Part of that is left over from the early spirit of the internet and the idea that participatory and direct democracy is a superior model to representative democracy. It generates an inherent confiict due to the idea that architects or planners somehow do not represent themselves and that is a primary reason to fight against them. But no!

Architects and planners have been chosen through a democratic system of public tender that belongs to the democracy. Finalists have been selected through election. People voted for these representatives at the level of your local borough or your city or your state and they have then appointed a specialist. To then ask very specific questions to a local population really values the work of the architect and the landscape architect, because otherwise we could very easily end up in situations in which we try to make ourselves disappear and we try to look like we are dissimulating our power and I think that's very dangerous.

Pooja Agrawal There is an ongoing tension between localism, the idea of protecting your back garden versus the idea of having an overarching strategy that considers the whole neighbourhood and city, and all its communities. Trying to mediate that can be quite difficult. Architects can be that mediator and I think you have an advantage in that you are not the local authority and are also not the local resident, so you are able to shape people's opinion and broaden their imagination.

Peter Swinnen I was expecting to hear you talk about the housing itself. Where is it now at? What kind of state of development is it in?

Mathieu Delorme We just delivered the masterplan.

Peter Swinnen It would be interesting for the sake of the discussion to show the real building and the related materials. It's an important part of the puzzle. At the moment I'm lacking this crucial information. We need this information to make a fair judgement for further discussion.

How do you keep the project in line with your first intention? How do you keep your ideals without being too disrupted by collaboration, participation, and related consensual attitudes?

We are not asking big questions. Citizens have to aknowledge that they gave power to certain elected bodies to make decisions for them about broader policies and the built environment.

Harriet Harriss Assuming democracy is necessarily participatory is a really fraught road to take. It's challenging to co-design projects with diverse communities when you have increasingly polarised politics – such as those who voted to leave Europe and those that didn't living in the same block or street. The people who can afford to participate are not always the people that represent their community well – they just happen to be available and interested, whereas others may have health issues or family challenges that limit their engagement.

Mathieu Delorme We are trying to make a fifteen-year strategy for local involvement with the city because the mayor understood that their methods have to change. It's brand new and the key point is the project house. It will be a place where people can go and we are allowed to follow them on the reconstruction of the building. But because it's a fifteen-year project the two first architectural building projects will be constructed by 2020. The last one will be completed in 2035. It's a long period of time, which is something we don't know exactly how to handle for sure. We try to go step by step with the public sector. We believe that in order to sustain the public's engagement and attract new people we have to create a micro-economy. How we can try to grab participative finance from people?

The idea is to create a shortcut in order to put individuals' money into the local economy instead of investing it into classic financial products. We try to make shortcuts between individual savings and the global financial economy. This money can contribute to making a communal forest, or more generous architecture with shared spaces, a loan system for youth entrepreneurs. We want to create more direct links to make people invest in local projects instead of fuelling capital investments.

I've seen so many tool kits, all sort of pedagogies, ways of creating a kind of Esperanto around participation and its methodologies. There seems to be no uniform, consensual or international language on how we do this. No community is ever fixed, but fiuid. So what kinds of activities can be implemented to enable those who come late to a project to have some kind of stakeholder infiuence over the outcomes?

Jack Self The institution that I'm representing is called REAL. One of the reasons for that is that I have a strong interest in material artefacts, in material objects of the built environment. It's quite hard to understand in real terms what it means for a local economy to take surplus savings from a population and then to use that as part of a local development fund in order to initiate a new local economy. But then you see something like the bench, you see something

We try to make shortcuts between individual savings and the global financial economy.

This money can contribute to making a communal forest, or more generous architecture with shared spaces, a loan system for youth entrepreneurs.

We want to create more direct links to make people invest in local projects instead of fuelling capital investments.

like the project house – the idea that you would preserve one of the buildings, rehabilitate it in order to be used as a focal point answers one of your questions, Harriet, about how you can create long-term engagement. It is such a simple thing that becomes an extremely important material artefact that signifies invisible structures.

Tiago Mota Saraiva I want to step back to the discussion on democracy. I'm in favour of the representative democracy but I think that you can only have representative democracy when you have both vertical and horizontal participation. For example, last year in Lisbon, during a general assembly on a mostly public social housing neighbourhood, a decision was approved: the municipality should not nominate Romany community families for vacant houses in that neighbourhood. This is a decision that goes against the law. The municipality has to say that the decision is not politically and constitutionally acceptable. We are always working with these top-down and bottom-up situations and it is important to understand that we need both in a democracy.

These last years of austerity have been based on ideas, beliefs and policies that are fundamentally against architecture, against design or against any discipline that tries to design for the future. Austerity is mostly being imposed through the idea that There Is No Alternative (TINA) – the idea that people cannot imagine or demand a better future. On architecture, design, or urbanism this attitude is against the discipline itself. The low-budget, temporary interventions made by collectives are in a certain way consequences of the crisis and developed in areas that are not really attractive for investors. So, because of the nature of the land we are working with, we deal with precarious conditions. My question is: how can we sustain these kinds of interventions? We started by reacting to a crisis situation but we must be more political and more involved on structural thinking. How can we affect the structural policies? How can we design a law? I will always reject seeing crisis as an opportunity. We have to structure our practice so that it can become something more besides being a temporary action for the crisis.

Austerity is mostly being imposed through the idea that There Is No Alternative (TINA) – the idea that people cannot imagine or demand a better future.

On architecture, design, or urbanism this attitude is against the discipline itself.

Alex Axinte & Cristi Borcan, studioBASAR

City School, Bucharest

Cristi Borcan, studioBASAR We first would like to introduce the context of Bucharest. It's completely different from the rest of Europe, especially London or a Western European metropolis.

We are an architectural studio and a public space practice. This mix is also because without our architectural practice we could not sustain projects dealing with the public space. I want to make this clear from the beginning: opposite from what was said earlier, in Romania there are few public funds for the kind of projects we do. We have one national cultural fund. Only one. And this influences fundamentally the way we practise, as you can easily imagine.

We develop a lot of actions in public space – they range from temporary to permanent. We use applied research, community activation, participatory programming, urban design, and live education programmes. We are trained as classical architects but none of the tools we are using in our projects were taught or learned in school.

We grew up during communism. But it was a completely different communism than our parents' communism. And that is because we were in our childhood and for us everything was like a playground, with a lot of freedom. There was a very good time for us, although public space was very controlled, and the state was very powerful, controlling every aspect of life. What happened during the 1989 revolution completely changed the paradigm of public space: people took action against the state – a phenomenon that didn't happen until then in Romania.

People took action on every part of public space and it was a strong moment of emancipation and freedom, especially for people who had spent their life in a socialist neighbourhood – which is basically everyone. These socialist neighbourhoods were built to fit the new socialist woman and man according to socialist ideology; they were not built only for social reasons. So, in Eastern countries, there is a difference between socialist housing and social housing. In socialism housing was for everyone. And they are still like that nowadays: the population is very mixed in these neighbourhoods.

After the revolution the massive protest against the state opened the way for a massive privatisation. The structure of the society and the morphology of the public space changed: most of the public facilities disappeared or were privatised – being turned into shopping malls for example; industrial areas were opened to speculation; housing blocks, parks, and leisure spaces became giant car parks. Our lives were directly influenced by the introduction of the capitalist Western mode of consumption, and it has influenced our work a lot.

After decades of socialism and forced collectivism there has been a rise of extreme individualism and privatisation at every level of society and the city. These phenomena are visible all around the public space: parking places on

MEGA IMAGE

sidewalks; fences around playgrounds and green spaces; individually thermo-isolated apartments; personal heating systems – because a lot of people want to be disconnected from public resources. Extreme individualism has led to general mistrust. This leads naturally to the loss of a public sensibility and public spaces.

Of course, there are also reactions to these changes and ways of living. Like in every extreme situation people find ways of surviving by collaborating: building small-scale furniture – benches, playgrounds or even water wells in front of their apartments; gardening in communal green spaces next to their blocks; or by acting: extending their apartments; transforming ground-floor apartments into small shops. This was important to explain because this context totally rooted our action and the project Alex is going to present.

Alex Axinte, studioBASAR The project Scoala de Oras (City School) is composed of different projects. It's a project created by Porsche Romania and developed together with Bucharest Community Foundation. It is a corporate social responsibility (CSR) project that was selected by an independent jury and awarded one of the grants in 2015. The project is still running.

Continuing into 2016–2017, the City School's subject is public libraries, aiming to activate public and community space through a live educational project. The Bucharest Metropolitan Library consists of a network of 30 branches that still exist as one of the last surviving networks that is producing and distributing culture and education. For example, in the socialist collective housing neighbourhoods it remains one of the last starting points of both spatial and functional potential to activate and coagulate the community. Basically, all the other public facilities are gone.

Working with the network of public libraries we discovered the peculiarities and interesting sides of this network. One thing is that they are site specific, almost to a chameleonic kind of specificity: different context – different library – different behaviour. This results also from the fact that only two libraries among the whole network of 30 branches were built as libraries, while the others were just located in leftover ground-floor spaces owned by the municipality. Even though there is a law that regulates the minimum number of square metres dedicated to a certain number of inhabitants, a study made by a Romanian architectural group called Collective East revealed that only 20 per cent of the necessary area is met.

Let's zoom in on a particular case in the neighbourhood of Militari. It is where we decided to focus our intention and we made a pilot project. Militari is an area of almost 300,000 people. It's a very densely populated neighbourhood.

It could be ranked as one of the largest cities in Romania but it's only a borough of Bucharest. The library is located on a ground fioor of a housing block, behind a very crowded commercial market that faces the boulevard. The library was almost invisible due to the fact that the windows are painted. The space was planned in the '60s as a communal living room because the block was made of one-bedroom apartments and tenants were in need of a room to meet with their families. The communal living room has been transformed over time for various uses and ended up being a library that had been closed for several years when we started the project. There is one more library nearby, so potentially they can function together.

We didn't invent a problem, but reacted to a very dramatic situation, related to the disappearance of the social space's most basic infrastructure. When we started to ask people during the research phase about where they usually meet with their acquaintances, one of the answers was in the supermarket. We thought that these existing public libraries in the area could play a social role.

Our main ambition was to transform the closed library into a social infrastructure. That is also why we decided to focus our interest on the public spaces between the libraries.

We wanted to involve students in the process in order to pursue our ambition of starting a live educational project. It is a way to introduce students to skills and knowledge they would never learn in the Romanian school system. We wanted to offer a real experience with the idea that education could be done through situations instead of being artificially created in a laboratory format. We pushed for having tutors and students from diverse backgrounds - from architecture, sociology, landscape design. We built partnerships and alliances with universities so that students receive credits for the work they do with us during these workshops. Students participated at every stage: from research to interviews to workshop organisation and of course to design and building projects. It was a fantastic experience for them and it was compelling to be part of such an experimental hands-on project, and to use a hammer. You never touch a hammer during your architecture studies in Romania.

The most important work is impossible to show through nice pictures because it is a history of building relationships. We also did physical interventions: we removed the paint from the windows; we built bookshelves; we developed a mobile pavilion and different sorts of urban furniture to create a more welcoming environment for the public realm around the libraries.

It is really important for us to upscale the lessons learned to the network of libraries. That is why we developed a guide that will help librarians to start a similar process in their branches.

Biblioteca
se
redeschide

The attitude of the project was to open up to the neighbourhood. We started by making questionnaires, interviewing the inhabitants, the neighbours, the former users of the library, the users of other libraries. The research and activation process was a sort of pioneer project for everyone involved – for us, for the students, for inhabitants, for Bucharest Metropolitan Library – they had never done this before. Even the financing partner was pioneering its relationship with the Bucharest Community Foundation. It was a first time for everyone.

We also organised a workshop for ideas with the librarians. We gathered to discuss their problems. One of the main issues was related to visibility. It sounds like a very short-term need: to become more visible in the midst of retail advertising that is savagely overtaking streetscapes. Scratching off existing layers of paint on windows was one of our tactics as well as using bright colours for the added public furniture to attract attention to the library. With these kinds of diffuse interventions, attentive to the need of librarians and locals, we created a neighbourhood living room. We organised in the library an exhibition about the neighbourhood's history. Some of these tools are used as mirrors, to show the face of the neighbourhood to people. Organising an historical exhibition about a socialist neighbourhood was something that people wouldn't think could exist, because they assume that the neighbourhood has no memory and that history only existed for the city centre.

We were also very open to suggestions. For instance, we interviewed people who had always lived there. They started to propose ideas about possible alternative uses of the library. We organised all kinds of meetings, DIY workshops, inhabiting the living room, organising screenings, hosting Christmas chorales and collective readings.

The goal of the project wasn't the reopening of the library. We wanted to locate a live project into a real space and Bucharest Metropolitan Library granted us the access. And then, asking people, opening doors, organising events, raising the question about how this library should be transformed, we created the expectancy. The management of the library realised that and made a huge institutional effort and reopened the library, equipped with a librarian, a daily schedule and some books. So by engaging and studying the subject we started to provoke and move the subject.

We also took the library out on the street through a mobile pavilion that we called Trailer for Research and Activation. We used it to announce the re-opening of the library and we also lent it to other institutions and groups that we thought could be interested in activating public space. The Metropolitan Library used it as a mobile branch for the three following months. Cultural associations that don't have these kinds of tools to go into public space have

used it. Civic groups have used it for organising pop-up events. It was used twenty times by different users over six months.

The CSR also launched an evaluation of our project. It was a very interesting moment when the Bucharest Community Foundation (FCB) and the CSR programme looked at the social return on investment (SROI). We were not familiar with such a method. Nobody was. Even for the CSR and FCB it was the first time they used this evaluation tool. It was a very interesting process because it consisted of interviews and discussions with the stakeholders of the project, which were the students, the librarians, and the team. So we had a lot of feedback on our project through the SROI and it was extremely interesting to collect all the points of view on such an action.

The evaluation process stressed also some of the associated risks represented by the super-monetisation of life, which is a scary phenomenon for us. But the process is still experimental and we try to understand the indicators and also try to learn a new language through the process. The collaboration with the CSR was also a rich learning process and we became familiar with the notion of the social value of the project. It helped us to see success and failure within the methodology of our project. According to the evaluator, it appears that the main beneficiaries were the users of the Trailer for Research and Activation, then the students, then the library management. The project team got a minus on the report so we apparently get no social value out of the project. It is a very interesting measurement tool in conjunction with the monetary tool, which together gives us an idea of how much an amount of euros invested is able to gain in terms of social value. These are policy indicators that refer to a professional policy language. It allows us to understand languages different from the one we are used to speaking. It opens new semantic fields for qualifying our process and projects, far from fancy professional magazines or internet popularity measured through the tyranny of likes on Facebook.

Melanie Dodd It's really nice to see live projects from a fresh point of view, I mean, from a context different from Western Europe. It makes you reassess what project-based learning is; you begin to understand the full network of implications. Some things work across a bigger bandwidth of knowledge – from using a hammer to understanding systems of governance. This is something that's embedded in parts of architectural education but is not fulfilling its potential and it is an answer to why architecture education needs to expand as a discipline. Architecture education is focused on subjects, which is always going to be necessarily small, whereas if it starts to cut horizontally across societal ways of working, then it suddenly opens up. I'm just reiterating this idea that you situate.

Another important thing that comes out of your talk is the idea that the university is a key partner. In these precarious times in which there is a blurring of what's public or private, how things are funded and how they work both in terms of governance and society, this idea that the universities are key partners to mobilise projects is really important.

Harriet Harriss What's compelling about this project is how effective deinstitutionalising architectural education can be. Thirty years ago, 80 per cent of university budgets would have been spent on academic staff, and 20 per cent on administration and management. In the thirty years since, we've managed to invert that sum. A university chancellor now demands a CEO's salary. In the UK, educators are no longer public-sector workers, we are instead working for the private sector. Within your model there is a latent ambition to disrupt this notion of keeping education as something that needs to happen within the cloister of a design studio or an academic institution. We might need to move towards these models due to economic circumstances and questions of affordability in architectural education, so do we need to modularise education around this kind of project in order to make it accessible? During this project, how engaged was the community in the building process – not just the architecture students learning how to use a hammer, but the actual community participants themselves in gaining architecture skills?

Alex Axinte Because the library had been closed, whatever coagulated around the library also disappeared. It's very interesting to be in a community when something disappears – all it takes is a few years for it to be like it was never there. It was very hard in just a few months – this was a six-month project – to get some of this awareness back. The students engaged the inhabitants in a consultation phase. If the project had spanned a longer period or if we had worked with existing civic groups we could have started from a different level of engagement. One of the most difficult parts of these projects is to crystallise a group around a topic. Doing this with students, we discovered things that are very peripheral and it's not a pedagogical objective. But for example, encounters between generations does not happen very often, but in these kinds of projects, because we are doing interviews and questionnaires, it happens more frequently. It doesn't fit within the objectives of opening a library, but to put retired people and young people in a conversation is important – there is no place in society for this to happen anymore. Working with students was the main goal, and then also working with some of the neighbours who were in a spatial crisis. This neighbourhood is very disconnected from the centre so

What's compelling about this project is how effective deinstitutionalising architectural education can be.

Thirty years ago, 80 per cent of university budgets would have been spent on academic staff, and 20 per cent on administration and management.

We've managed to invert that sum. A university chancellor now demands a CEO's salary.

residents can't go to the centre to use public facilities; they are kind of imprisoned in the neighbourhood.

Harriet Harriss If you look at the etymology of the word 'participation', it means 'to share' but it also means 'to take'. And obviously what has been taken in this project from the student's perspective are vital architectural skills relating to community engagement. But it would be quite useful to also up-skill the community participants as part of this installation. Architecture skills will always be relevant to these kinds of spaces in order to maintain them and to allow people to shape them in the future. But if students' involvement is tied to an academic timetable and they engage in communities in a short-term way, it becomes a legacy challenge. In some ways it can disrupt relationships and stop the project from developing. Equitable skill-sharing – for example, making sure the community get as much from it as the students do – is a particular challenge that I've faced in some of my projects and seems extremely present in this one as well. Without the students driving the project, will it still thrive?

Alex Axinte Yes. We face that issue. We realised that we relied on students a lot – we've asked for too much time, too much engagement – for a project that is not included in their university credits system. That is why we went to the university to create a strategic partnership that would allow students to receive credits. It was an interesting discussion about how our live project could be seen as a pedagogical exercise.

Peter Swinnen You mentioned Porsche Bucharest.

Alex Axinte It's a car dealer.

Peter Swinnen I presumed so, yes. (*Laughs.*) Porsche is a big player, right? I have a lot of respect for how you try to manage the project and hold on to it, and push it as far as possible. But I would expect that there is a discrepancy between this big player and you guys – scratching the fioor and the windows. Did you manage to convince them to enhance their financial contribution for the coming years and involve them much more in the project process? CSR can't be an excuse for big companies to do something small and ethically good. Did you manage to make a difference on that level?

Alex Axinte This CSR is managed by the Bucharest Community Foundation which is one of the most innovative NGOs in Bucharest. By attracting private

Corporate social responsibility can't be an excuse for big companies to do something small and ethically good. Did you manage to make a difference on that level?

money and channelling them towards funding NGOs or groups of citizens on different topics, they created this project. It was an ideas competition with an independent jury of professionals who were not only from Porsche or the Bucharest Community Foundation. It was a big event in our very small scene. As we said, we have only one cultural fund that holds one or two competitions a year.

Peter Swinnen My question is: do you have tangible evidence that this project actually succeeded in convincing them to enhance the CSR impulse?

Joachim Declerck I have the same question. We have been involved in similar kinds of projects where there are great moments when things start to work and then there is also the moment after work when you ask yourselves: how did this incredible energy you spent and invested change the logic of things? Did it lead to a multiplication? Did it change the way the library system functions and is operated? Did it change how Porsche operates? The way the Rockefeller Foundation has changed from sending out money to engaging around topics? Did you have the feeling that you were changing certain logics?

Alex Axinte For the first time in this project, the Metropolitan Library invested public money in the refurbishment of the space. They replaced the windows and they made a bathroom; until then it was only the CSR funding.

To make a social return of investment evaluation was something that had never been done before in a CSR in Romania. The Bucharest Community Foundation convinced Porsche to participate for a second edition. It is not like the Rockefeller Foundation that gives grants for many generations. We participated in the first edition. Bucharest Community Foundation convinced them to contribute again because of the results of the five CSR projects that were supported. They then contributed to a second edition with increased budgets. Our project was invited to continue for the second edition without participating in the competition. We realised from the analysis of the SROI that you can't just do a six-month project and quit. You have to follow-up with a second edition to guarantee the quality and sustainability of the projects over time. From that point of view, our small project managed to change how the CSR worked.

Flavien Menu Our student from last year, Arya, spent a year studying CSR in Belgium.

Arya Arabsh The CSR is a really fascinating regulatory resource. It has a lot

We realised from the analysis of the social return on investment that you can't just do a six-month project and quit.

You have to follow-up with a second edition to guarantee the quality and sustainability of the projects over time. From that point of view, our small project managed to change how the CSR worked.

of potential but it comes with a price: usually the investor wants its own image to be promoted. I'm really surprised that you managed to invest a lot in the local social fabric. Usually the CSR tries to target a larger audience afterwards or at least promote it. Usually investors want to have their branding on it. I was wondering if you can explain how you managed to work over this confiicted situation and if there was any promotion afterwards?

Alex Axinte No, there wasn't.

Arya Arabsh What was Porsche expecting?

Alex Axinte There is a website. Again, the biggest player was the Bucharest Community Foundation who was filtering the process. You have to place the CSR in the context of Bucharest. For example, this project had a budget of 10,000 euros and for the second phase of around 8,000 euros. I don't know if this sum is small ... but for Bucharest it's very big. You have to imagine that there are few municipal or government funds.

Peter Swinnen Did you invest money in this project?

Alex Axinte As a team of coordinators, yes. The CSR limits the amount you can allocate for administrative costs – 20 per cent of the total – and of course we needed more than 20 per cent. But just a few years ago we worked for free in this kind of project, so for us it's a step forward. It's also a step forward for our students. It's also a step forward for the libraries. It's a big step forward for the CSR and for the Bucharest Community Foundation. We were aware of the risks as we saw extreme monetisation of the social return on investment. But, how much does a smile cost? The ones who are doing the evaluation process are very aware of this metric.

Pooja Agrawal Public funding often works by saying, 'I'm going to invest 200,000 pounds and from that we want 20 jobs, 2,000 square metres of public space, and so forth'. This is seen as a valid output or outcome. However it is increasingly important to have a conversation about social value. What is that? How do we define that? And I'd like to understand a bit more about how you define it in your project. Did you define it before you started? Is it something you understood along the way? And how did you measure it?

Alex Axinte First we had objectives to target because it was a competition.

Public funding often works by saying, ‘I’m going to invest 200,000 pounds and from that we want 20 jobs, 2,000 square metres of public space, and so forth’.

This is seen as a valid output or outcome. However it is increasingly important to have a conversation about social value. What is that? How do we define that? And how did you measure it?

During the project we learned that we were going to be evaluated on those objectives. One of the objectives was to expose students to participatory projects, also to produce the trailer and make sure that it is used by different organisations, and to deliver a process to the Metropolitan Library that they can spread through their network. These objectives were successfully achieved and the evaluation was quite positive.

In the second phase we also had objectives, and some of them were remains from the previous phase. Now that we are more aware of the importance of evaluation we are thinking about how to evaluate our projects. It could sound like an excuse, but we are acting in a very small scene and whatever you do is considered great, everybody taps you on the back if you do whatever, because you are not quitting this kind of practice. In this context, it is hard to stay objective about the quality of our projects. The evaluation protocol was the first time that somebody asked us questions about what we got out of the project. It was also the first time that someone came with a methodology for evaluating us, by interviewing the students separately from us to understand the positive and negative aspects of the work.

Peter Swinnen I question the idea of the CSR because I think the CSR model could be something to activate education and not just a method for big companies to sleep at night.

Tiago Mota Saraiva The project showed the power that research can have in revealing what everyone has in common with other people. In this kind of project, people meet and talk and get in conflict. We shouldn't avoid conflict in our experiences of participation. We step forward when getting into conflicts. People start to get to know each other. The enemy starts to change its face – it is no longer about neighbours or strangers but it can be much more constructive.

I don't think the money Porsche or Bucharest Community Foundation invest will change the way institutions are working. They clearly know from the start that the small amount they invest won't change their image. But this is not important. What is important is the way you build alternative projects and the way you use it. From volunteering to grants, you have to be increasingly transparent about your fees, about how much it costs to make social actions and movement. That's the key issue. That's something that we have to dispute, make them understand that we are working mostly for the common good.

Jack Self I wanted to pick up on the point about how you measure value. I'm very sceptical of attempts to commoditise or to value things that previously had

We shouldn't avoid conflict in our experiences of participation. We step forward when getting into conflicts.

People start to get to know each other. The enemy changes its face – it is no longer about neighbours or strangers but it can be much more constructive.

no value. Of course traditional capitalism needs to calculate profit. And in order to have profit you have to have a measurement. So metrics are integral to this but often incomplete as soon as you start to say 'how much a smile costs' or 'we want to promote the value of inclusivity'. What I like about this project is that all of the value that is non-monetary is indirect or in fact shielded or concealed from the corporations and the CSR project through either material or indirect processes. You have the Bucharest Community Foundation which becomes the face of the project. Then you have all the projects underneath which are then shielded from that. So the CSR looks just at the foundation and you can create a website, you can do publicity, but all the projects underneath become invisible.

Flavien Menu What strikes me is the budget given by an actor like Porsche. For such a company, 10,000 euros is almost nothing while for you it represents a lot. So yes, it is a win-win situation but in the meantime it is a lot of reward for Porsche in terms of image and reputation – and probably in terms of tax exemptions. It reveals a glass ceiling, where this kind of budget is relatively important for designers but for bigger players it is pocket money. It is essential to learn and reach a certain level of economic and political knowledge. It allows us to break glass ceilings and be able to infiuence change at broader scales. Otherwise it makes us seem weak and viewed as little players.

Markus Bader I would like to add to that. Most of our projects are publicly funded, and mostly with cultural funds. There is an interesting gap when we sometimes have to disguise our work as art or theatre or through some other discipline. However, there is also an interesting gap that I call 'urban practice' which probably encompasses the funds that you were accessing and using for the project with this 20 per cent limit for administrational work. The framework completely lacks the idea that there is a professional doing the work. We are working somehow in this gap to create imaginaries or to translate a need or a potential into an activity or into a next step. In Berlin I started arguing for 'urban practice' to be included in the discussion whenever cultural funds segment disciplines.

Alex Axinte In the second part of the project, the administrative funds increased to 40 per cent. It is the direct result of the efficiency of our actions. This is something that we have done for many years: convincing through action. We cannot do this in a two-hour meeting. We convinced them by the first stage of the project that human resources are equally important compared with the physical output.

It is essential to learn and reach a certain level of economic and political knowledge. It allows us to break glass ceilings and be able to influence change at broader scales. Otherwise it makes us seem weak and viewed as little players.

We know how to wear different hats. We spread our infiuence through architectural pedagogy, through art galleries, or into urban administration. It is not very straightforward and I don't know if we are a movement – I never thought about it – but we are in movement all the time, acting and then thinking.

Bucharest encourages this because you have to do things – saying something is not enough because there is no one listening. We have to educate all these partners: the civic partners, the institutional partners, the financial partners, and the professionals that have never done this kind of project before. So how should we do it? We have to act.

Melanie Dodd If we think in a very forward way, it is important to consider that there is a social, large profitable top layer which is a redistribution of that down to people. It's interesting to think about that rather than to monetise every single thing you do. There is a blur between what you pay for and what you do as part of what might be a future non-work economy. It's worth thinking about, especially in light of where these funds come from and the objectives that they carry with them. Because if it's scalable to a slightly more radical level then maybe these are the ways in which things get done. We can rather think about how individual practices make economic models work; it's a completely different paradigm shift in how we operate.

Jack Self The next stage I can imagine for a project like this is to say: how can this not be a question of charity? How does this turn into the generation of local revenue? In the West we have hundreds of years of economic development that occurred in Romania in only twenty years. It therefore becomes much more extreme. But in fact, in nineteenth-century Britain there was no welfare situation whatsoever and there were a number of private associations, institutes and foundations that were set up and they were then nationalised and the process of nationalisation allowed them to then be privatised and sold off and destroyed. What does socialism look like after the welfare state? Part of that is of course creating a system that is robust enough to resist exploitation by larger forces. At a very small and simple level it can be switching between always being a consumer to generating value by yourself.

Mathieu Delorme When you were talking about value and measuring social value, it made me think that we have to think about currency. We value this with the euro. We have to think that our currency is a social construction, an economic social construction, and we have to maybe create a local currency.

It is important to consider that there is a social, large profitable top layer which is a redistribution of that down to people.

It’s interesting to think about that rather than to monetise every single thing you do.

There is a blur between what you pay for and what you do as part of what might be a future non-work economy.

In Nantes for example, we had a discussion about the involvement of the local people, asking how we could pay them for their work. There is a local and complementary currency in Nantes called the Sceau-Nantes. Maybe we can try to build a micro-economy based on this currency; we can explore and be inventive and make our own economic system for territorial and urban projects.

Jack Self We have to be very careful about those types of systems. In London you have initiatives like the Brixton pound. It is effectively a kind of microscopic economic protectionism. Of course the initiative is very clear in a moral and ethical sense: you have money which is not staying in the local economy and there is no incentive for it to remain in the local economy. So you create a system which artificially creates an incentive to prevent the money from leaving the local economy. In the long run, the ideological consequence is that you say there is no necessity for the universal and there is therefore no responsibility of either the state or larger-scale entities in order to effectively manage how economic resources occur. In that sense we have to be very careful where we locate the responsibility for these things because it should not be the responsibility of a local city to have a parallel currency to the euro. In that sense it is the responsibility of the entities responsible for the euro itself to ensure that the distribution of currency within society is more equal.

Holly Lewis I want to go back a little bit to something that Flavien said earlier. You said that we are small players, and I reject it.

Flavien Menu It was provocation, and I was surprised that no one reacted to it!

Holly Lewis If we accept that, then we are shooting ourselves in the foot and taking the money out of our pocket and it's nonsense! We have to not be small players. The city isn't a small player and construction is an enormous part of the economy! There is so much money being made and put in different pockets and sent in different directions and architects don't engage with that level and it's stupid. We have really great intelligence about cities and how cities come together and how people come together. We need to engage with those conversations. We need to try and direct them. We need to put ourselves in those rooms. We need to not be small players because the subject matter that we are dealing with is not small.

There are loads of examples of people who don't let certain perceived limits just be there. Richard Rogers, for example, said 'I'm going to be at that table, I am going to infiuence policy and government', and it is possible to do that. I

We have to not be small players. The city isn't a small player and construction is an enormous part of the economy.

There is so much money being made and put in different pockets and sent in different directions and architects don't engage with that level. We need to engage with those conversations.

don't believe that there is a glass ceiling. I think we need to get in the rooms and it is possible to do that, we just don't talk about it enough.

Pooja Agrawal That's one of the reasons why I joined the public sector. I wanted to be able, as an architect, to influence how money is being spent, where it is being spent, how much is being spent, who it is being spent on. As a student I was never exposed to the idea, that as an architect I could work in the public sector. And yes, funding for the public sector has been diminishing but we can still influence by being at that table and I think we should be more creative about what we can do as architects. This is why I am co-founding a new social enterprise called Public Practice that will place the most talented architects and planners in local authorities to work for the public good.

Joachim Declerck I think it's important to say that it's not the only option. We can read the world as 'there is big money being spent and we need to follow where the big money is; there is a lot of power that is still public, we need to go to the public'. The example of Bucharest is an example where a lot of the power is also in setting up initiatives – making a setting where things can come together and build their own logic. There is another capacity of design that can be used to design the logic to not scale up. A public framework might allow for many local initiatives, but that is a side of the design work that I think is crucial if we want to produce intrinsic meaning and capacity. That's where we have to really sit and discuss. That requires money. That requires a space that is hard to construct. However, that space allows us to design not the exceptional fantastic demonstrations and not the visualisation of the existing power structures but the new middle that can connect those two logics, the urban programmes, which is very hard but crucial to our ambition. If there is a movement, it is the movement to design logics out of the things we learn from these exemplary projects.

Flavien Menu We are living in the myth of public power and the phantasm of what public power is able to do. It's part of the public sector to work with the private sector. In France, for example, all the policy makers work with these consultancy offices – Deloitte is everywhere, it's at the Elysée, at the ministries, it's at the mayor's office and lots of other institutions. The private sector influences the public sector a lot. The limits of public and private, and good and bad, are blurred; there is a grey zone where we can intervene.

Jack Self I want to just say something very quickly to the students and the audience about Instagram because we live in an area in which there is personal

We can read the world as 'there is big money being spent and we need to follow where the big money is; there is a lot of power that is still public, we need to go to the public'.

The example of Bucharest is an example where a lot of the power is also in setting up initiatives – making a setting where things can come together and build their own logic.

brand, which is a completely different type of personhood in the world from natural human personhood. It doesn't really have anything to do with who you are. It has to do with the way in which you present yourself. Presenting ourselves as big players has to do with public perception.

For example, I will not tell you how many people work for REAL, although it's more than you might imagine. I won't tell you what our turnover is, although it's more than you might imagine. I do, however, feel totally comfortable going into meetings with Pricewaterhouse Coopers or with the Greater London Authority. One of the things that I resisted during my own education was when people would say, 'Well, this is an interesting architectural project for a student'. I think that when you start studying architecture you become an architect effectively almost immediately. If we look at how famous architects' projects are often looked at, people still talk about Rem's student work or Zaha's student work as being architectural projects. They are not student projects they are architecture. In that sense, as soon as we are taken seriously and begin to project an image of being capable of engaging with any level of society and any scale of project in any way, we also take the skills that we have as a discipline more seriously and thus we maximise our agency in the world.

Arya Arabsh Jack talked about monetising the smile, about what the next step would be after the charity level, and we also talked about how we can be bigger players. Something that is crucial here, as your office is doing, is to engage with this language. How can we learn the language of measurement? How can we build the language of measurement? There is an urgency to explore other ways of practising. For instance, the infrastructure sector is evolving a lot through the help of CSR and we should be able to infiltrate that market to take action. There has been a huge increase of attention in that sector in the past three or four years. By better engaging we can become larger players.

Joachim Declerck I agree, but we should not underestimate the fact that we can also set the language. I want to give one example with the term 'productive landscape'. It's an old term that hadn't been used for a while and at a certain moment the idea of the productive landscape as a policy programme came about. And now it's something that starts to rule by itself. It produces new commissions and the commissions are no longer 'can you redesign the landscape for agriculture?' or 'can you solve the problem of biodiversity next to the agriculture?' – no! – it is now, 'can you redesign the productive landscape?'. To set the tone to build a narrative of what we are talking about is a crucial step in making things spin by themselves. I'm always worried when we try to speak

We are living in the myth of public power and the phantasm of what public power is able to do.

The private sector influences the public sector a lot. The limits of public and private, and good and bad, are blurred; there is a grey zone where we can intervene.

the language of others. It's much more intriguing to find a language that conceptually triggers many parties. Both physically and linguistically.

Holly Lewis It's also extremely gratifying to hear politicians use a term that you invented!

Peter Swinnen The re-emergence of the term 'productive landscape', at least in Belgium, was unsolicited. It's nothing new but it brings together a lot of energies that already existed and all of a sudden it was formulated in such a way that in five minutes the minister could understand the potential impact. He could understand the huge potential for future policy. Again, in five minutes time they are willing to put a lot of money on the table that you can use to set up pilot projects.

Alex Axinte We do not think of our project as simply making a nicer library with new furniture, but it is rather a prototype for a new type of institution. Even at its small scale, it's a prototype of an institution. It could scale up. It could go into a network and can be replicated, it can be copied. And then it's a big project. Small players make big projects, if they work together.

Flavien Menu Pooja and Holly hold key adversarial positions within public and private institutions and organisations. The role held here is different from the one in an architectural project, but it helps to sharpen one's capacity to speak with decision makers.

Anthony Engi Meacock Returning to the question of education: there is a lot being said about the essential understanding of your agency and your position in the world. What wasn't discussed is the idea of opening your mind through live projects. You start to understand your role in educational models by doing things and you start to understand the power of your agency. That is never discussed in architectural education. By doing something you have a drop of power but you also develop your own sensibility. To talk about these things is to take responsibility for putting your ideas into the world.

Joachim Declerck The question of education always leads to the question: do we have a new model of what the architect should be able to practise? The question of movement is the same question for me. I liked what you said very much: we are moving. I don't think we should fall into the trap of trying to define what the architect should be able to do. I don't think we have a movement.

We do not think of our project as simply making a nicer library with new furniture, but it is rather a prototype for a new type of institution.

Even at its small scale, it's a prototype of an institution. It could scale up. It could go into a network and can be replicated, it can be copied. And then it's a big project.

Small players make big projects, if they work together.

What is happening is that many offices are doing very different things, but they start to function together.

You can emerge from an architectural education and choose very different types of practices according to your own capacities and interests. But we should try to define the new architect not as a kind of total figure, but rather find ways to connect forms of architectural practices.

I was educated in the Netherlands and in Belgium. Belgium has no overarching vision in terms of architecture education. The Netherlands only has overarching vision. Which one is wrong? You need both! The Netherlands is trying to find a way to come to concrete projects that are qualitative, that make sense within a larger vision. Belgium is trying to make a larger vision out of a lot of projects. They both need the same capacity. They need the way to link those two and I think that's something that we really need to think about. How you curate? Connect these different forms of practice – the temporary, the more persistent, the more infrastructural, the intervention, and so on – in a movement. Because then we have a movement.

Alex Axinte Do you think that schools can be big players?

Joachim Declerck Yes. I think in the Belgian and Dutch context the schools are bigger players than the cultural institutions. An enlightened minister founded the Dutch Architecture Institute, the Berlage Institute, and secured the funds to stimulate architecture and the Rotterdam Biennale. These three institutions have defined the context of Dutch architectural production for the last twenty years. They made platforms for cultural production and the budgets to test things. And are they doing the same now as twenty years ago? Not at all. The current cultural practice is that of trying to pool and curate connections. It's an infrastructure, you could say, for the grey space.

Peter Swinnen I do believe educational institutions are not taking the question of what they could do seriously enough. There is still this kind of lingering undertone of what an ideal practice might be, of what a canon might be. The educational institute has a huge responsibility in raising awareness for future practitioners, which it is not taking up at the moment.

There is an interesting gap for architectural education to actually jump into a grey zone – to make sure that practice and education become much more of an intimate couple. There is not one way of practising.

Tiago Mota Saraiva I think we should avoid the idea of new architecture. We

I do believe educational institutions are not taking the question of what they could do seriously enough.

The educational institute has a huge responsibility in raising awareness for future practitioners.

There is an interesting gap for architectural education to actually jump into a grey zone – to make sure that practice and education become much more of an intimate couple.

are talking about extending boundaries. I don't like to see it as a movement but more as a collaborative moment that is changing the way of conceiving our discipline. I was taught that you start a company after working for a famous architect for ten years. For me this is a totally obsolete model. Today we are proving that obsolescence by sharing our thoughts, our experiences. We stopped competing and started to understand that our practices can be symbiotic. I can take something that Anthony told us today and try to apply it to an experience we're having. In the end we should be more cooperative than competitive. Once we were all running for the same competitions, we were all running for more or less the same work. Right now we are creating our own work but also trying to understand from each other how to improve it and how to open new doors for our practices.

For example, Alex and Cristi open doors by engaging this process of the CSR. It might also open new doors for other people in Bucharest or Lisbon. It is not a canonic movement but a symbiotic accelerator based on sharing, debating and discussing arguments that can add value to our practices.

Melanie Dodd I think you can be disruptive on many levels. Students need to learn that small-scale disruption is valuable – even if larger scale disruptions may have more agency in the long-run. The field of action is something that you step into the minute you start an education and maybe the time has come to deregulate the architect and the methodology of sticking with one route, which may in fact ultimately be counterproductive.

We should avoid the idea of new architecture. We are talking about extending boundaries. Today we are proving that obsolescence by sharing our thoughts, our experiences. We stopped competing and started to understand that our practices can be symbiotic. I can take something that Anthony told us today and try to apply it to an experience we're having. In the end we should be more cooperative than competitive.

Anthony Engi Meacock, Assemble

Granby Four Streets, Liverpool

Anthony Engi Meacock, Assemble I'm a part of Assemble. We are a collective of fifteen to nineteen people, depending on the criteria you use. We came together to build a single project which then started a collective working practice. I am going to talk about a collection of work, not a single project. The work is situated in Granby, which is located in a central area of Liverpool. Its growth was directly connected to the docks, and as a result it was one of the first true multicultural areas of the United Kingdom – through the docks, beginning in the nineteenth century, a huge infiux of Somalis and other migrants came to the area. It had a really vibrant political scene; it was where much of the support for Nelson Mandela came from in the United Kingdom.

The area had a very active life, but one that was quite challenging to the status quo. Deindustrialisation of the city and the port had a heavy effect on the area. Things came to a head in 1981 following the closure of the ports and a huge rise in social problems. Ignited by an incident of police brutality, the area erupted in a series of outbursts that have been described as race riots. But when you speak to people there who lived through this period, they characterised the riots as based much more on class, as the area is very mixed ethnically and racially.

The response from local and national government, rather than tackle the social problems that had resulted in this mass disenfranchisement: poverty and crime, was to essentially clear the area and break it up. This is a map showing the areas identified for demolition. These four streets are the last surviving original houses and this is where our work is focused. This was in 2007 – the council forced out the residents and planned to demolish the area to then rebuild lower density housing that would have increased value, under a scheme called 'manage decline' – which is as negative as it sounds. Obviously, the key thing missing here is the idea of civic functions within the city. The council rebuilding programme was exclusively focused on the implementation of housing in a suburban model with no proposals for replacing shops, pubs, schools – or anything that could maintain the existing communal infrastructure.

Granby Street is the main street that dissects the whole block. It was a really vibrant high street that was intentionally destroyed except for a tiny cluster at the northern part. This cluster, which was empty, still retained a civic structure and appearance. The result of this clearance – quite predictably so for us – was that crime did not go away, gang activity increased in the vacuum.

In recent years, this council policy has been accepted as a mistake, which presents an opportunity. We entered the scene when this moment of failure happened. Because the waves of development from the 1980s and 1990s had really failed to deliver on their social promises, that had driven up prices and

LIVERPOOL

ECHO

www.liverpoolecho.co.uk

NEWS/SPORT/LIFE. IT'S HAPPENING 40,321 MAIN EXTRA Monday April 26, 2010 49p

Shots fired

TWO streets in Toxteth were cordoned off today after reports of shots being fired.

Officers were called to Longfellow Street at around 11.50pm after residents heard a number of loud bangs.

There were no reports

● Turn to Page 5

SEALED OFF: Longfellow Street

'BUS SMASH' HOUSE HIT AGAIN! Page 3

GERRARD
We can't let Blues finish above us Back Page

RUSH JOINS REDS
Legend back at Anfield – Page 43

MIKEL KEEPS EURO HOPE ALIVE
Sport Extra

WE LEFT STREETS LIKE WAR ZONES

EXCLUSIVE
City leader admits housing blunders

REGRET: City council leader Warren Bradley

by DAVID BARTLETT
City Editor

LIVERPOOL council leader Warren Bradley today vowed to turn around the city's derelict communities after admitting they were left like "war zones".

Cllr Bradley said the council's housing policy – and that of its partners – had "ripped the heart" out of communities.

He was speaking about the flagship Housing Market Renewal Initiative (HMRI) which is costing tens of millions of pounds.

In a frank interview with the

● Turn to Page 6

WOMAN HURT IN ARSON TERROR
Story – Page 12

demand, left crime to itself, and avoided creating any kind of social infrastructure, the council was interested in trying something new.

Here a group of residents remained – mainly those who owned their homes, partly driven by the fact that if everyone is forced out of the area, suddenly your house is worth nothing and you can't get out, partly as it was a place where people had grown up – about ten on the street. And in response to an extreme situation of deprivation they were taking matters into their own hands from the local council's total abdication of social responsibility. Instead of being tired of looking at empty streets, the residents painted the window frames and houses so they didn't look empty anymore. The council has a habit of demolishing buildings for no real reason, so this graffiti appeared as a kind of joke – and protest – as if the council would knock the buildings over by mistake.

The idea of this small axis of agency, a small axis where you can take control, increased the value of a place that is viewed as having no value. We also tried to change the perception of the site, making a project distinct from the council's approach.

After a series of unsuccessful attempts to solve the crisis in the area and a series of broken promises by developers, the residents felt unheard and distraught. When we met them it really felt like an opportunity to help make something happen. People in the city have a huge amount of power if they take it. But often the system tries to ignore or suppress that power. We worked with the residents to develop a strategy of incremental improvement using the small pockets of funding available; what emerged was a masterplan and co-inhabitation of the street for an extended period of time.

This is a post-rationalisation drawing showing the activities at our adopted base – number 48: the front room was used by the builders when the building started happening, the basement was used as storage for the street market and to help the gardening, the back garden served as a kind of impromptu workshop for a collaborative project making items for the houses, and we stayed in the top fioor. Here we regularly met with the residents to collectively develop and evaluate the development model for the area – documenting what was valuable, what was functional, what was really successful there, and also documenting the failures, the obvious problems.

This was a strategy where, instead of a tabula rasa and the hope that somehow a community emerges, you build from the amazing existing social infrastructure – a far more piecemeal, careful and incremental way of building. This is the idea of accretion that enables a much more gradual development means that you can adapt, change and evolve as you go.

The residents established a Community Land Trust (CLT) and secured a grant from the National Lottery Fund, which enabled us to access further grants

from the Homes and Communities Agency, the council, and other charitable loans. This funded the restoration of the first ten houses. The aim was proving that, while these houses were not financially viable to restore in a normal development model and that the council was giving them away for a pound, we could do these up for very little money and far less than a new-build would cost.

This was a very careful, slow approach with a lot of compromise. We tried to keep the identity of the houses through low-cost interventions. This does not mean that the quality is not good, it simply means that we can do a lot with not so much.

For example, we kept the pitched roof structure that gives the house a charm that a spec building would never have, took care in the choices of materials and focused effort on those extra bits – that we refer to as embellishments – that can transform a very pragmatic, even boring shell into something that could be thought of as a home. And that could also take on the character of the people moving in – something they could identify with. Moreover, the series of products and items show that love has been taken in the process. We provided a complementary set of skills that are different from what you find among the residents and helped provide the extra bit of energy to bring ideas to fruition.

We have a strong belief that the functioning of a city relies on more than housing alone. You need civic functions, shops, etc. Here the production of 'embellishments' slowly evolved into the opportunity to create local economic activity, which led to the Granby Workshop.

The Turner Prize offered the opportunity for large exposure and secure funding for a new social enterprise. The products that were designed for the houses – sometimes with the residents, sometimes with people in Liverpool – are produced in Granby both taking advantage of existing skills and training new skills. They are for sale, initially during the Turner Prize and now available online. The income is reinvested in the neighbourhood – the ambition is to create a new business in the area that functions within the city. It is now in its really early stages and I don't know if it will necessarily work but the indications are positive. The series of products are very much about revealing the hand that made them – a series of processes where the handmade is manifested. You are aware of the method they were made with – you have the printed fabric, the pressed ceramic, the lights, the wood-fired doorknob... they all leave a distinctive idea that these things are not necessarily expensive to make, but there is an understanding that these are made by individuals who have their own kind of agency.

This is a piecemeal development where housing comes first and it then generates interest and new money comes in. The workshop was then set up to exploit that and now, in the middle of the site, you can see the glass roof, where

we are working on a project which explores what communal infrastructure can be. You could call it a community centre but one that isn't cheap and miserable and based on a logic of economy that feels very false. In fact with the same economy you can build something extraordinary.

An image had existed for a while when we opened the door to one of the houses and there was a tree growing in it. Gardening and other collective activity has been incredibly beneficial, and so a space that supported those activities in the area seemed very important.

We also had an opportunity as two houses had been omitted from the original restoration work; rebuilding them wasn't economically viable because they were in an advanced state of decay. Here again, it is thanks to the publicity and the media and political focus on Granby that we have been able to get further funds and to establish a different economic model to refurbish these two houses into an extraordinary communal space – and one that is not only dependent on public subsidies.

We secured Arts Council funding to deliver a new type of space: one that provides a connection to the past by showing the past reality of the houses. At the same time, the project will, through hosting a series of residencies, support the symbiotic working relationships (like the residents and ours) that have been deeply beneficial in delivering the work in Granby. So this space is also a look to the future. One house remains totally open as the garden space. It is a space where you might have a children's birthday party one day, a market happening the next day. The other house functions like a meeting room, and on the first floor above it is an Airbnb type of space that enables both a collective guest house for the whole street or for practitioners, artists, etc, to be invited to the area. It allows for the continuation of this symbiotic relationship where people with different practices can work in the area. By trying to gather people and energy, you can create a more resilient structure.

This is the garden space and the common room, which reveals the studio behind the bedroom. These spaces provide enough income from exploiting opportunities for artist-led investment, which is not cost-neutral but starts paying for other improvements in the area. That's the hope – to incrementally improve this area through an approach we feel is valuable and is applicable to other spaces and other places.

Kathryn Firth Does your job ever finish? You have taken a mentoring role that ties into the issue of attitude and role of the architect. The word 'architect' seems to be insufficient in describing what you are doing here. One could see your role carrying on forever. What is the end point? Gentrification?

ARTIST-IN-RESIDENCE'S BEDROOM
CHAMBRE DE L'ARTISTE EN RÉSIDENCE
BATHROOM
SALLE DE BAIN

AEM I don't know when we finish. The idea is that we actively employ people in the workshops and steadily withdraw, so they end up being in the director's seat. Gentrification might be a real issue. In this case you have to raise property prices, because they had no value, but slowly to avoid displacing people. This was something that the CLT was really aware of as well. They inserted a clause in the sales contracts for the properties that owners can sell it only at a rate that is tied to the median income of the area. In terms of the effect more widely, it is probably acting as a gentrifier for properties around it. But it is difficult to know exactly what you can do about that. As long as you are conscious you can mitigate as best as you can. It might be a disaster, it might be gentrified and be really horrible. But it feels too early to assess.

Pooja Agrawal When you were first approached, you probably didn't know what you were going to do. I guess the whole idea was that you were writing the brief with the clients. The architect/client roles were slightly more blurred than usual and over time you developed the scope of the project. My question is: how do you make this sustainable? I am guessing you do not fill out timesheets.

AEM Actually we do. We are a business, we get paid, we charge fees. We try and divide the work and we are very conscious of what can be exploited for more money without being a problem, and we do that. The CLT is really good – they pay us, they think the work has value, so it wasn't ever really a challenge. The residents were quite forthright: 'You have to get paid! We do not want to exploit you, come on, invoice us!' For the Winter Garden we worked very closely with other people to secure the funding from the Arts Council, so we took a bit of a risk, but compared to a competition it was a way lower risk than entering a competition with a brief that is written beforehand. The problem with competitions is that the briefs are often shit. Here we get to write our own brief, so we had so much control that it actually makes it far lower risk than some traditional architecture practice.

Audience The project seems to have a certain element of condescension because you are all upper middle class and you're coming from a certain educational background and then you go into a deprived area. And the aestheticisation of the documentation of the process raises the question of how far this has become part of the construction of an architectural career. With the Turner Prize your practice has gone up in the market, you've gained value in the market of architects. What was your approach in the participatory process with the community, what was the exchange? Because the doorknobs, etc, have

something a bit exclusive to them. Did their situation really change? Are they politically activated?

Jeremy Till As a person who has been there several times I would say: don't get too distracted by the doorknobs because they are a fraction of the process and the really interesting stuff is the legal and tenure side of building community interest and convincing the council to give this entire street to the residents. That's where the project is for me – not the tiles and the doorknobs.

AEM It's probably better to ask the residents about their situation rather than me, because I am obviously always going to say that it's great. Yes we are a bunch of very privileged people and I guess the question is can you use that privilege in different ways for good or bad – you can try to do something you believe in. Often people get criticised for being privileged and having the audacity to think that they can do something positive, which I think is unfair. Here we have tried to use the privilege we have to positive effect – and how successful that is, is how it should be judged

Jeremy Till When you were presenting the staircase it struck me how classically architectural that was: why don't you present the project as a set of spreadsheets? Because that, for me, seems to be what your amazing skills are – to actually manipulate spreadsheets rather than to manipulate the doorknobs.

AEM That's ... yeah, it is a really good point!

MATCH
Reebok
Carlsberg
Reebok
Carlsberg
FOWLER & McMANAMAN
liverpool

Jack Self, REAL

Real Review, London

Jack Self, REAL We have been talking about a methodology of designing with time and through time as an intrinsic role of the architect. And in that sense it would have been appropriate for me to present *Home Economics*, which is the British Pavilion at the Venice Biennale this year, which I curated, and which was designed through time and really tries to look at this.

But I decided not to do that! I decided to present a magazine, because for me there is a crucial importance to spread messages conveyed by our generation to a broader audience. There is a lot of value in saying, 'We believe in democracy, in inclusivity, in equity; these are the values that we stand for and we'll try to pursue them through the material evidences of our work'. It is capital to do so if we want to resist the crisis of the left, this crisis of lack of belief, this kind of agony of power that Jean Baudrillard would call anxiety about privilege. The right don't suffer from that – they're conducting revolutions, they're taking Britain out of Europe, they're building walls, they are locking Europe. In that sense it's equally important to design a door handle and to design a spreadsheet or masterplan.

The *Real Review* comes from the REAL Foundation. I don't trust myself and I don't trust other people; I start from the basis of an alter-neoliberal doctrine which is that no one gets out of bed in the morning to do things unless they have an incentive. Let's assume that that's the case. It's rather reductivist but as you get older, as you get fatter, you get comfortable, you get tempted to follow the money, you make a series of decisions and quickly you find yourself sliding in a direction that your young idealistic self would reject but you say, 'Well, it's not so simple actually, I was really naïve back then'.

How can you take these alter-neoliberal values into the structure of an architectural firm? The way that we did this was by creating the Real Estate Architectural Laboratory, or the REAL Foundation. It's structured using the same model as the Architectural Foundation in the United Kingdom – it's a limited company. It has articles of association which are published on our website and make available the types of projects we can do. We have a group of advisers who in some cases might reject a project because it doesn't fit those criteria. I'm the director; in the future I could stand down and someone else could replace me and the essence of the company would remain the same.

We do many things and these articles of associations dictate a certain way of working and therefore we don't draw any distinction between publications, exhibitions, building projects, etc, – they all are scales of the same ideas.

In Venice this year Patrick Schumacher said to me, 'Architecture is like a Ferrari. It's so expensive that most people, if they ever buy one, they only buy one in a lifetime, and it would be the single most expensive thing they do'. And

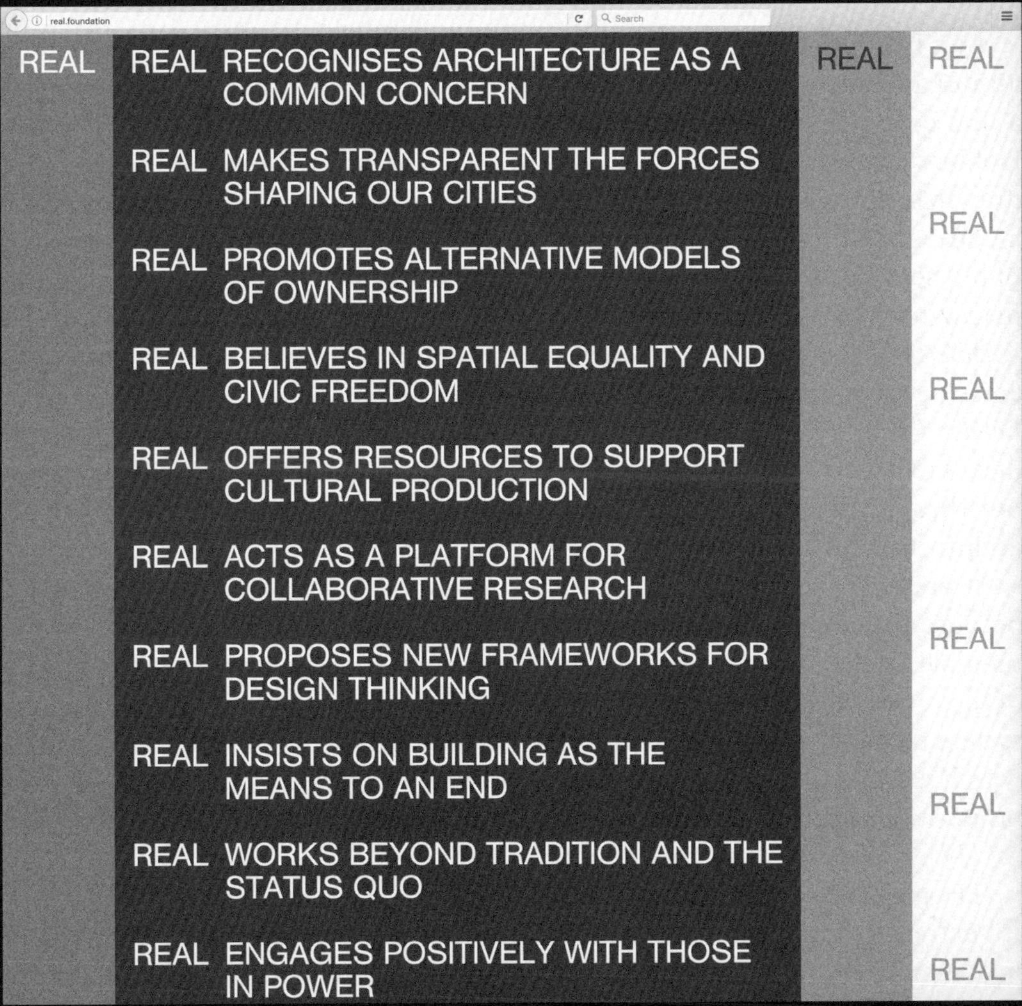
real.foundation
Search
REAL
REAL RECOGNISES ARCHITECTURE AS A COMMON CONCERN
REAL MAKES TRANSPARENT THE FORCES SHAPING OUR CITIES
REAL PROMOTES ALTERNATIVE MODELS OF OWNERSHIP
REAL BELIEVES IN SPATIAL EQUALITY AND CIVIC FREEDOM
REAL OFFERS RESOURCES TO SUPPORT CULTURAL PRODUCTION
REAL ACTS AS A PLATFORM FOR COLLABORATIVE RESEARCH
REAL PROPOSES NEW FRAMEWORKS FOR DESIGN THINKING
REAL INSISTS ON BUILDING AS THE MEANS TO AN END
REAL WORKS BEYOND TRADITION AND THE STATUS QUO
REAL ENGAGES POSITIVELY WITH THOSE IN POWER
REAL
REAL
REAL
REAL
REAL
REAL
REAL

I said, 'Well, you know, Ferrari also makes hats and t-shirts and key chains', and he replied, 'Yes, that's why we make tables'. But Zaha Hadid tables are still like 2,000 to 20,000 euros each. So my question to him was, 'How do you create an ideological keychain? How do you represent the essence of Ferrari as an ideology at the scale of a small industrial object? How do you create architectural ideology which can work at the scale of a global vision for the future of the world and something extremely modest, a sheet of paper? How do you work across those?'

Our fiagship magazine, *Real Review*, was funded by a Kickstarter campaign – almost a thousand people collectively pooled 23,000 pounds – which is why on a first cover we featured an image representing our interpretation of Thomas Hobbes' Leviathan with a dozen people exiting from his mouth: a symbolic drawing expressing the power of bringing people together. It was started with a colleague of mine, Shumi Bose, who left REAL before the first edition was published, but she was very instrumental in setting up the structure of the magazine. The *Real Review* came out of the fact that I was reviews editor at the *Architectural Review* and then they stopped publishing reviews. Day one, the concept for the magazine was, 'We will just review books; it will be like the *London Review of Books* for architecture'; day two produced the slogan, 'What it means to live today' – it's a review of the contemporary. It is a review of everything but through the lens of architecture, through the particular way in which architects think.

It presents a series of reviews. The concept of the review is very important because the review looks back in order to look forward. It's grounded in the tangible, in the material, or in things that already exist. Today, we tend to think of the review as being a literary review, but the review spans from the Amazon system through to the academic review. The review asks, can we examine things which exist in the world and find a potential in order to create a positive proposition? I think this is an intrinsically architectural way of thinking because we always have to come up with a proposal.

The magazine presents long-form articles and it's aimed at a general readership. It's extremely important for me to win over the general public. I always think of my mum. She's a really intelligent women; she is not disinterested in architecture – she knows who Le Corbusier and Mies van der Rohe are. She quite likes Charlotte Perriand but that's pretty much it. But subjects like Henri Lefebvre's concept of the production of space or Karl Marx's class struggle as it existed in Red Vienna are impossible to get across to a general audience. Although there are so many interesting things in architectural culture today, they remain contained within a very introspective discipline. So the idea of mass communication is

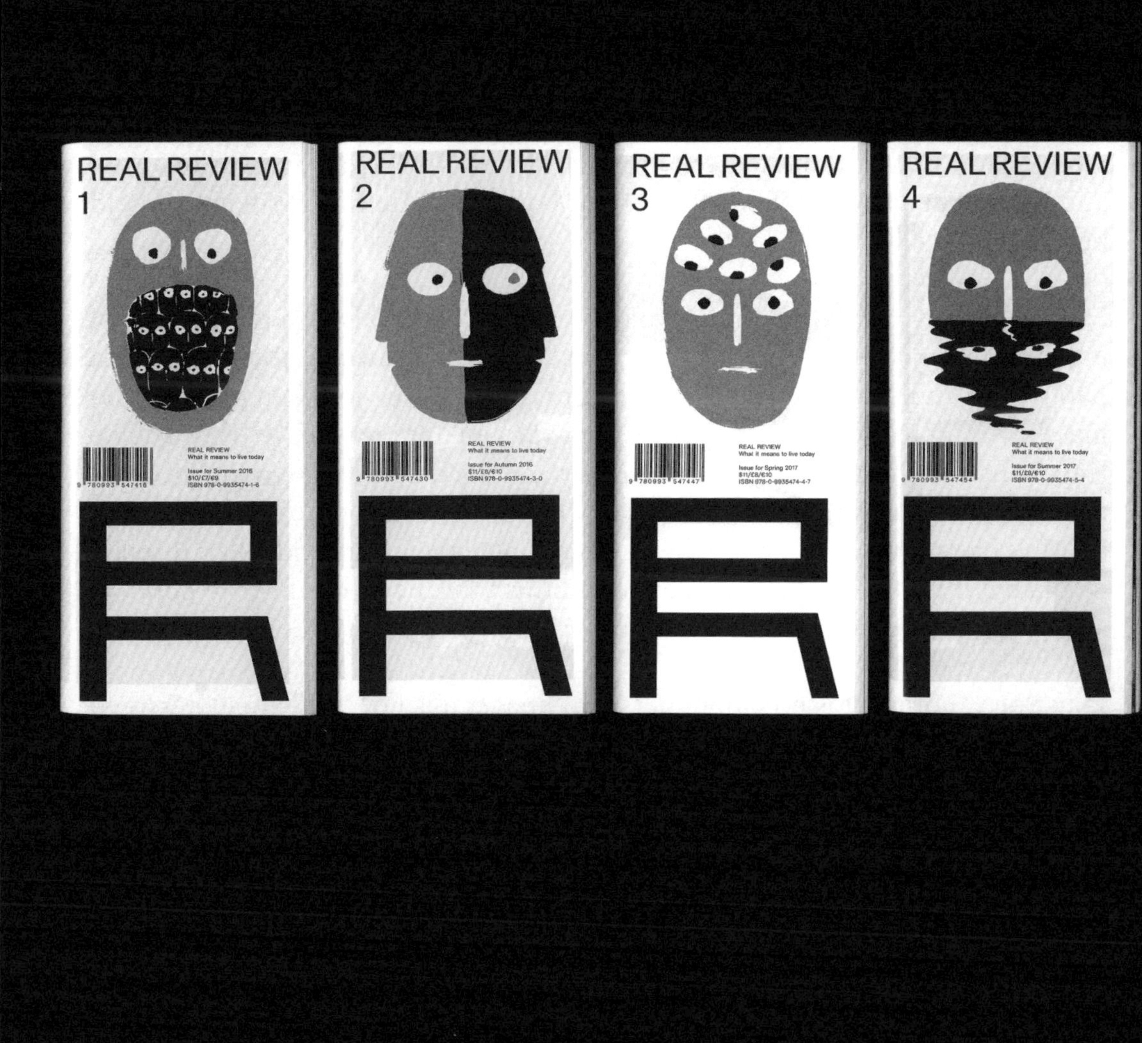

REAL REVIEW
1
REAL REVIEW
What it means to live today
Issue for Summer 2016
$10/£7/€9
ISBN 978-0-9935474-1-6
REAL REVIEW
2
REAL REVIEW
What it means to live today
Issue for Autumn 2016
$11/£8/€10
ISBN 978-0-9935474-3-0
REAL REVIEW
3
REAL REVIEW
What it means to live today
Issue for Spring 2017
$11/£8/€10
ISBN 978-0-9935474-4-7
REAL REVIEW
4
REAL REVIEW
What it means to live today
Issue for Summer 2017
$11/£8/€10
ISBN 978-0-9935474-5-4

very important. The point of the review is to then interject and say, what is the space for changes within this?

'The only thing stopping you is you, trying insane to remain the same. This pretty much is the motivation.' This is a nice piece by Reiner de Graaf from OMA. I'll end on this piece. Reiner de Graaf explores an intricate history of concrete panel housing and concludes with the fact that he grew up in a mass-housing complex near the port of Rotterdam. Family members would come to visit and they would say, 'It's fairly inhuman, fairly annihilating here, I don't understand how you could all live in this'. Whereas for him and the people that lived there, there was a lot of comfort in the material equality and the fact that all the houses looked the same; they didn't see that as an aggregate of individual houses but a single block that represented the entire groups of people that they knew lived inside. This shows a very strong and intricate relationship between the material reality of how we live and the immaterial and theoretical ideas that we have about how the structure of society should be. Thank you.

Flavien Menu I want to discuss your use of media. You have a real control of media, of your own image – you mentioned earlier in the day that you have a public face and a private face – and it's quite interesting that you speak about mass communication. It's also a way to promote your own image. People take leadership roles by shaping their image through media. Here it has allowed you to successfully crowdfund thanks to subscribers and followers. You revealed an invisible mass of actual people. Millennials promote their work and image through media but it is also used by people around this table here to infiuence political and economic decisions. How could mass communication become a weapon?

Jack Self For us, it is not about personal image; it is not at all about personal brand. And, in fact, the insistence on the consistency and uniformity of what is produced is really an attempt to resist anything which suggests that it's about one individual. It is also important for REAL to develop a specific aesthetic which is replicable in an attempt to be in a way ultimately generic and also recognisable so that you can associate particular ideas and ideology with that visual media.

Oliver Wainwright I have a question about audience and your idea of mass communication. Your audience by definition is going to be self-selected because it's a crowdfunded magazine. How do you get around that, how do you reach an audience outside the kind of people in this room?

THE FINANCIALISATION OF HISTORY
Sam Jacob

If this text were a documentary film, we would begin with a shot of the green-brown water of the river Thames lapping against the alginated stone embankment outside the Houses of Parliament. We would zoom out, while fading to spliced footage of two boats on the river. One, a grainy video, would feature a punk band. The other, more professionally produced, an heir to the throne. The editing would make you feel that these two boats, though distant in time, were somehow occurring in concert. That these two Thames trips were speaking to each other. That the Sex Pistols Jubilee year jaunt, and Prince Charles' "Vision of Britain" were part of a continuous flotilla that began in 1977 and ended in 1988. Or rather, a period bookended by these voyages that continues to shape us.

that in the establishment of the Historic Buildings and Monuments Commission in 1983 (soon more snappily renamed and now simply called Historic England).

The National Heritage Act did two things. It first consolidated the various heritage functions of government into a single, smaller, more "efficient" entity. Secondly, by establishing it as a quasi-autonomous non-governmental organisation ("quango"), it also became a commercial entity, producing its own revenue streams. Instead of primarily being concerned with preservation, as it had been, English Heritage was dedicated to the commercial exploitation of state-owned historic properties. In broad terms, this was the privatisation of history.

"History" in the 1980's was subject to the same ideological transformations as other economic sectors. As the heavy industries that had defined Britain since the Industrial Revolution closed, history became one of the new post-industrial products.

In place of industry and manufacturing, Britain became a pioneer in the post-industrial products of finance and history. We didn't sell things any more but ideas, concepts that took the form of financial services and historical experience. History was re-imagined as a commodity that could be mined, refined and traded. Heritage became a resource, a function of financialisation.

And just as the transformation of financial services through privatisation, deregulation and the Big Bang had created strange immaterial financial products – derivatives, futures and other instruments that liberated capital from their bounds – meaning and value became increasingly dislocated.

Financialisation equally transformed history. This newly imagined idea of history began to do more than simply narrate. Instead, the fantasies of historical England began to merge with its real artefacts. Real castles became historical theme parks where fictions merged with history. Bejerkined out-of-work actors dressed up as knights and friars at abbeys and palaces. Visitors could participate – churning butter in the kitchen, holding out an arm for a hawk to sit on, firing an arrow – in ways that made them feel that history was coming alive even as it became theatre. History shifted from fact to experience, entertainment and engagement. Across the country, historical sites became scenographic, where the big-screen fantasies of historic England could be collectively performed.

As these remakes and re-enactments played out across the country, nostalgic fantasy became rooted too in the heart of Government. Performing rituals of nostalgic Englishness became far more than play, much more than fantasy. Re-enacting myths of nationhood acted as a very real mechanism of radical ideology.

In this new idea of what history was and how it could be used, architecture found itself centre stage. Architecture became factory where new historical product could be manufactured. Its fantastical theatre of

THE FINANCIALISATION OF HISTORY
Sam Jacob

If this text were a documentary film, we would begin with a shot of the green-brown water of the river Thames lapping against the alginated stone embankment outside the Houses of Parliament. We would zoom out, while fading to spliced footage of two boats on the river. One, a grainy video, would feature a punk band. The other, more professionally produced, an heir to the throne. The editing would make you feel that these two boats, though distant in time, were somehow occurring in concert. That these two Thames trips were speaking to each other. That the Sex Pistols Jubilee year jaunt, and Prince Charles' "Vision of Britain" were part of a continuous flotilla that began in 1977 and ended in 1988. Or rather, a period bookended by these voyages that continues to shape us.

The 80's revival endures into its 3rd decade, with no sign of its wheel spinning any slower. With every rotation dizziness blurs any real relationship to fact. Instead, its very repetition becomes the thing that is repeated. Its signs and symbols continue to spin on an ahistorical Catharine Wheel, spewing coloured sparks into the night. That the 80's, above all decades, should remain in this perpetual state of re-performance is no accident. It is the moment where culturally and politically the idea of the past-as-future emerged. Between John Lydon's searing scream of "No Future" in the Sex Pistols God Save The Queen, through to Prince Charles' "Vision of Britain" and Francis Fukuyama's essay, "The End of History" (published in 1989) something very strange happened to history, perhaps to time itself.

In the late 1970's and early 80's a new form of radical Conservatism emerged. Part of its radicality was the sheen of nostalgic ideas about England. Thatcherite Conservatism promised two things: That everything would change, but that everything would also stay the same. Britain would be entirely remade according to free market principles, deregulation and privatisation, and in doing so, Britain would re-enact itself as a Great-again nation.

The political landscape was defined by the dream of a frictionless, efficient private sector future, freed from the postwar social settlement. But this futuristic dream was simultaneously festooned with the imagery of the past. The future, under Thatcher, became a complex and contradictory idea. No longer the futurist white-hot heat of Harold Wilson, but a supercharged dream of the past. The defining moments of the era – the Falklands War, the Big Bang and the Miners' Strike were all washed with the flickering glow from the perfect screen nostalgia of *Merchant Ivory* and *Brideshead Revisited*.

This obsession with history, greatness and nation is in part explained by Thatcher's own obsession with Churchill. History, Churchill tells us (and her), is written by the victors. But he would say that wouldn't he, as both victor and historian. Churchill's obsession with history was a primal force in the way he manufactured his own present, drawing on the past as a guide, as a source of intelligence, comfort and warning.

But Churchill's historiographic view of the world began, after his death, to consume the world. Once Churchill had become history himself, the image of him as wartime leader assumed a new significance. Churchill – the Churchill of bulldog spirit, of fight-them-on-the-beaches, of a Britain that was both victorious and still imperial – was raised as the ghostly muse and protector of British Conservatism. This ghost of Churchill was recruited most clearly in the Falklands War. Thatcher, many argued, manufactured the conflict just so she could appear Churchillian: a real battle acting as a re-enactment of an occult sacrifice to raise the spirit of history within her.

Nowhere more was this contradiction at the heart of Conservatism between history and the future played out

that in the establishment of the Historic Buildings and Monuments Commission in 1983 (soon more snappily renamed and now simply called Historic England).

The National Heritage Act did two things. It first consolidated the various heritage functions of government into a single, smaller, more "efficient" entity. Secondly, by establishing it as a quasi-autonomous non-governmental organisation ("quango"), it also became a commercial entity, producing its own revenue streams. Instead of primarily being concerned with preservation, as it had been, English Heritage was dedicated to the commercial exploitation of state-owned historic properties. In broad terms, this was the privatisation of history.

"History" in the 1980's was subject to the same ideological transformations as other economic sectors. As the heavy industries that had defined Britain since the Industrial Revolution closed, history became one of the new post-industrial products.

In place of industry and manufacturing, Britain became a pioneer in the post-industrial products of finance and history. We didn't sell things any more but ideas, concepts that took the form of financial services and historical experience. History was re-imagined as a commodity that could be mined, refined and traded. Heritage became a resource, a function of financialisation.

And just as the transformation of financial services through privatisation, deregulation and the Big Bang had created strange immaterial financial products – derivatives, futures and other instruments that liberated capital from their bounds – meaning and value became increasingly dislocated.

Financialisation equally transformed history. This newly imagined idea of history began to do more than simply narrate. Instead, the fantasies of historical England began to merge with its real artefacts. Real castles became historical theme parks where fictions merged with history. Bejerkined out-of-work actors dressed up as knights and friars at abbeys and palaces. Visitors could participate – churning butter in the kitchen, holding out an arm for a hawk to sit on, firing an arrow – in ways that made them feel that history was coming alive even as it became theatre. History shifted from fact to experience, entertainment and engagement. Across the country, historical sites became scenographic, where the big-screen fantasies of historic England could be collectively performed.

As these remakes and re-enactments played out across the country, nostalgic fantasy became rooted too in the heart of Government. Performing rituals of nostalgic Englishness became far more than play, much more than fantasy. Re-enacting myths of nationhood acted as a very real mechanism of radical ideology.

In this new idea of what history was and how it could be used, architecture found itself centre stage. Architecture became factory where new historical product could be manufactured. Its fantastical theatre of

Jack Self When we completed the crowdfunding we had 860 subscribers and since then its growth has been quite surprising. We have enough money for six or seven issues because of the independency and stability of the subscriptions-based financial model.

In terms of the audience, I try to promote it in the most diverse circles as possible. For the first issue we printed 4,000 copies and they almost all sold; we now have 2,000 subscribers and it's growing. For the third issue we will have a distribution deal that will take our print run up to 7,500, which will make it the largest architecture magazine in the UK by circulation. Now if you look at the people who subscribe, a third of them are from the world of fashion, about a quarter are from the world of design, and the remainders are a combination of the general public like my mum's friends – who backed us on Kickstarter – and obviously a high number of students in architecture and architects. My ideal subscribers are *Daily Mail* readers.

Oliver Wainwright How do you engage with them? What is your tactic to reach the *Daily Mail* reader?

Jack Self Well, I haven't got to that one yet. (*Laughter.*)

Pooja Agrawal Do you tailor your content to target that audience? Because a 10,000-word article by Reiner de Graaf about concrete housing doesn't sound like something for a *Daily Mail* reader. How much do you compromise the things that you might be interested in, to target that audience?

Jack Self Well, you have to have a mix of different content; this is an editorial question. There are two aspects: one is, what type of question do we want to produce, and then, what are the core ideas that we're trying to promote and what is the best way to promote them. How do we take these ideas and make them engaging and entertaining? It always starts with an ideological position. But it's also a question of the writing. There are not bad subjects for writing, there are only bad writers. And a lot of my work involves defining a very basic editorial structure: there are no sentences more than 25 words long and we use a fairly reduced vocabulary to avoid any type of jargon at all.

Jeremy Till Can I ask a question about representation and identity? This table of critics is different from the audience in terms of its composition – in terms of gender, ethnicity and class. Jack rightly got a lot fiack for the issue of *REAL* in terms of its...

April 20th 1945: The Red Army advances towards Berlin. It's the Führer's birthday, but there is little cause for celebration. Shots can be heard inside the city. In the Führerbunker – the command centre of military operations – confusion ensues. The Russians hold a railway bridge over the Oder, and are firing long-range artillery. A phone call to the front breaks rather more disturbing news: it is not long-, but short-range fire. The Russians have taken up positions at Marzahn, 12km from the city centre. A few days later, the Russians have progressed further. After a long rant about the supposed betrayal of his generals, Hitler concludes, "it has become impossible to lead and the war is lost..."

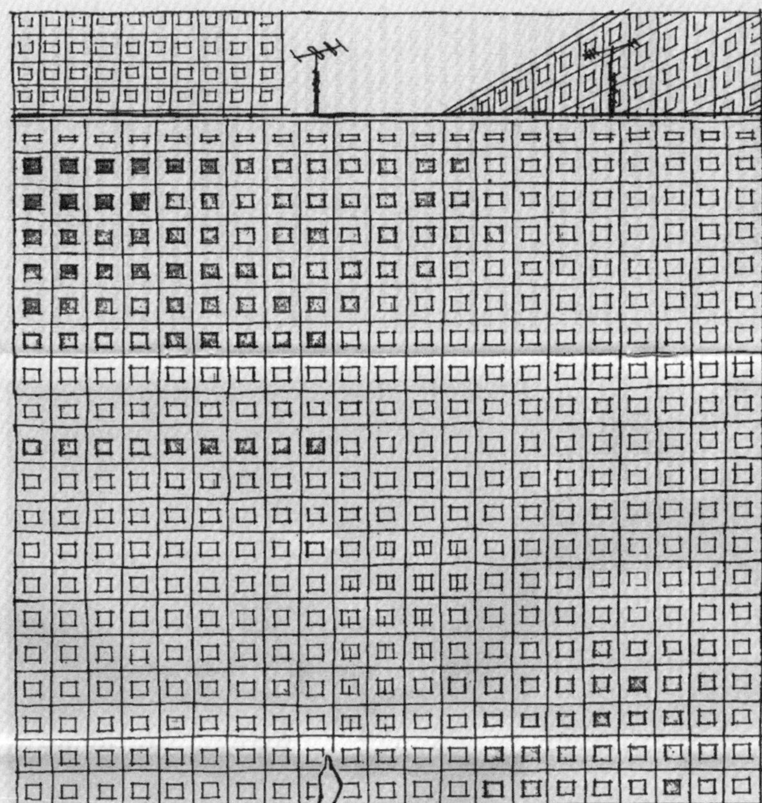

"Say hello to your grandma, she's seventeen windows from the top and two hundred forty-seven along."

Jack Self ...overwhelming white, male representation.

Jeremy Till Full disclosure, here I am: probably the best paid person in the room, went to Eton and Cambridge, am white and male, so probably not quite the right person to ask this question. But how can we have political agency when we are so unrepresentative of the audience, of the constituencies that we should be working with?

Jack Self The first issue was actually an accident. I commissioned 50 per cent men and 50 per cent women and through a series of extremely unfortunate and totally unrelated events, nearly 60 per cent of the women who were commissioned didn't file or were unable to file. And then we had an agonising decision about whether we should delay or what we should do about that and in the end we published anyway and decided that we would face the fiack.

The fiipside was that almost all those pieces by the women we commissioned came in like three weeks too late, which would have made the second issue 80 per cent female. But we decided to turn it back to make the balance 50–50. But those kinds of number games are not important for me. For example, there is a piece by a male author which is extremely pro-feminist. When we were talking about what it means to be European, it's also extremely important in *Real Review* to reach beyond the Anglo-Saxon world and to reach beyond the traditional subjectivities that we listen to in our English-speaking environment. There is an attempt to straddle the line between what you might expect and what you don't expect. And to present things that people are really eager and find easy to read with things that they might find more challenging but which might also change their opinion.

Pooja Agrawal I think the issue about how you reach a diverse audience is by making sure that people around the table are diverse in terms of gender and ethnicity. The idea that this magazine would reach someone who reads the *Daily Mail* or my auntie who lives in Dagenham – there's no way she should ever want to read that magazine. Recognising that fact is bolder than saying that it's actually for everyone. Saying that it is for people who study architecture, who are generally middle class, that's fine. Recognising that we live in an echo chamber, that's more powerful than actually saying that you think it's for everyone across class, gender and race.

Jack Self I think the aspiration is important, because if you abandon the aspiration to be inclusive, then you really are in an echo chamber. I make this

Millennials promote their work and image through media but it is also used by people around this table here to influence political and economic decisions. How could mass communication become a weapon?

magazine not just to try to present ideas to people who already agree with my positions or have a framework to understand them, but also in order to create new audiences and to expose ideas to other people. My aspiration is to make something that is as accessible as possible.

Kathryn Firth You said your mission is to create a magazine that reviews things through an architecture lens. There are many different kinds of architects – are you representing all of their lenses, corporate included?

Jack Self What I can say is this: there is a small group of readers in Sydney that I studied with at architectural school, who do not come from wealthy means, who are doing a lot in their local condition to try to change the way that architecture operates. It's an audience that I would not normally be able to communicate with, and I feel that it's very important to have such a geographically diverse audience. On the other hand, one of the vice presidents of Condé Nast subscribed, so the scope is wide but it's also not up to me who chooses to subscribe. All I can do is try to promote the values that I have – which have to do with inclusivity, equality and democracy – through editorial and the design of the magazine. I can only do the best that I can.

Peter Swinnen We are talking about a new generation putting out a magazine, which is obviously putting you in a lot of financial stress. Maybe there are other means – quicker, less expensive means to put out this content to a much broader audience. To be honest I don't know what I should take home with me, from what I've heard from you. I heard a very good promo-talk, fantastic; it is your project so you're going for it, fantastic ... *et alors*? I think you need to give us a bit more of this extra value that you try to put out there.

Jack Self Two things. First about why it's a magazine. It creates huge authority and validation from the authors who are published and printed. It still has that value as opposed to a non-print publication, and that's very important for me. In the previous incarnation of this magazine, which was a student magazine at the AA called *Fulcrum*, there was a single line on the middle of a single sheet, with two articles by two very different authors on the same subject. There was always a plurality of voices, but also you would have someone who is very famous often published next to a student or next to someone who had never been published before. And that creates democracy. In *Real Review* you also have very well-known people next to someone who has never been published before, side by side, and that authority is very important for me. That's what editing means.

How can we have political agency when we are so unrepresentative of the audience, of the constituencies that we should be working with?

There is a cost per square metre in a magazine in the same way there is in buildings; you prioritise by what you include or what you exclude, which means there is a finitude to the magazine as a proposition.

But in terms of my takeaway, it's extremely simple, and I will give it through the following metaphor: my parents were ill suited to each other as a couple and divorced when I was ten. One of the things that triggered that divorce was the fact that we had a circular dining room table. My father comes from a very traditional middle-class British, white background, my mum comes from an Australian background in which she was working class and a very vocal and strong feminist. And I think my father struggled to find his place in the family when he was not at the head of the table but in fact on an equal footing with his wife – not his wife, she refused to marry him – his partner and children. Now, what that tells you is that the head of the table is both a literal and metaphorical concept – it is literally just the head of the table but it has a metaphorical value as well, showing power relations, showing economic and cultural power relations that manifest, that are enforced and reinforced, through the material environment.

That's why we are called REAL. Because it's really an insistence on the fact that you can alter ... there was a fantastic experiment in the 1980s by a group of suffragette architects – not even architects – designers in America who changed the path between the head of the table and the armchair next to the fireplace in houses that they were designing, so that line passed through the kitchen and the laundry, thereby revealing and making visible the otherwise previously disguised labour of wives. It sounds really minor, and maybe even twee, but it is actually very powerful that such minor conditions of space, minor alterations of space, have huge impacts on social power relationships.

That's the content of the magazine, which we didn't discuss that much. These stories are about looking at the things which are everyday, banal, and which we take for granted, and seek to understand how they enforce and reinforce social power relationships. Are these relationships that you believe in and support, can they be challenged? What is the proposition for that? How do we move forward on that point? That's the essence of the magazine; to take that idea to as broad a section of global society as possible is the ambition. That's it.

These stories are about looking at the things which are everyday, banal, and which we take for granted, and seek to understand how they enforce and reinforce social power relationships.

Tiago Mota Saraiva, Ateliermob

Terras da Costa, Lisboa

Tiago Mota Saraiva, Ateliermob I'm going to focus on a project that we started in 2012. It is sited in the outskirts of Costa da Caparica in Portugal. Terras da Costa neighbourhood is a fifteen-minute drive from central Lisbon. The site is a shantytown and next to it are massive upper mid-class building blocks. The distinction produces a natural confiict between these urbanities.

When we first visited it, it was clear that we would be intervening in a situation that presented conditions that are not proper for anyone to live in. Houses with no ventilation, isolation or natural light; no tap water; no legal electricity; no paved streets. On the other hand, the plot had high urban restrictions. It is labelled as both an agricultural and ecological preservation field. We set our goal on fighting for building new decent houses, on an urban plot nearby, but not on restructuring the existing houses, which generated the first confiict with some organisations that were on the field claiming to keep the people there and merely fighting for a few building improvements, although keeping the brutal social gap.

After the first visits we declared: 'We do not see the proper conditions for human beings to live here so, if you agree, we may help you start a common political fight to build a decent new neighbourhood for you' – we have always been political in our actions, and our political drive was heightened in 2011 when Portugal suffered the troika's interventions (a period of time when Portugal was under a severe austerity and privatisation programme imposed by the European Central Bank, IMF, a European Commission). There was an urgency to act for human rights.

But how did we get to this neighbourhood?

We started working in Terras da Costa through an *Universidade Autónoma de Lisboa* workshop called Noutra Costa dedicated to think the future of that territory. The decision of the group we were tutoring was to focus on what we could do with the people that live there in the present moment and near future.

We used the weeklong workshop as a starting point for immediate initiatives. We tried to organise a football match that might connect inhabitants with people that lived around the neighbourhood (none came!), design some benches and tables and ending up with a party. We tried to initiate a thing that did not exist – and exists with difficulty now – that is, to mix people from outside of the neighbourhood with inhabitants. Despite that, the football match coupled architects from the workshop and people from the neighbourhood and was actually the most successful initiative in this regard.

Afterward the locals came to us saying, 'We want your help – the issue is the tap water'. In the beginning we were saying, 'We can help you as citizen-activists but not really as an architectural office. Providing tap water is not a matter of architecture'. And in response they suggested the design of a community kitchen.

JOGO DA BOLA
TERRAS DE LELO MARTINS
sexta feira 29.06.2012 19.00 H
Noutra Costa Workshop Da/UAL - Ceact/UAL

This part of the process was bottom up, because building a community kitchen was the dream of one of the first and oldest inhabitants, Dona Vitória. Furthermore, they already had the tradition of eating together.

The project started with a series of failures – submitting a lot of applications to support the kitchen project and construction, and being denied. For one and a half years all of them were refused. At a certain point we met with a group of people that was working ten kilometres from our site, the French/German collective Exyzt. They were building Casa do Vapor, a temporary structure in a fishing village.

At the end of their project, Alexander Römer, now from ConstructLab, called us saying they wanted to give us the wood so that we could start building the kitchen. We wanted to have Exyzt or ConstructLab in the project but they gave us the contact of a similar Portuguese collective that was starting. That's how our partnership and co-authorship with Colectivo Warehouse started.

We tried to implement a participatory design process but the locals were always asking, 'When does the tap water arrive?' This is very relevant because you have to set basic conditions to start a participatory project. We had two questions about the kitchen that we needed the community to decide on. Is it going to have a closed, lockable area? They decided yes, it should. And where are we going to build the kitchen? They proposed a place that was one of the most tense areas, and they wanted to build there in order to occupy it and create a common space there. At a certain point of the discussion, everyone wanted everything to be contained in this kitchen – even a morgue.

But this community was indeed always under threat – the drug dealing networks, the police, etc. The police interventions were aggressive. It is no longer happening because now the community has relevant access to the media, which they can use to advocate for themselves. It's a matter of visibility.

Back to the economy of the project. We started with the support of Casa do Vapor, but then a person from a jury that was reviewing one of our applications contacted us. She was from the Calouste Gulbenkian Foundation. She wanted to understand the neighbourhood and our work and advised us to apply directly to them for funding. Our application was accepted and Calouste Gulbenkian Foundation supported a significant amount of our work and project.

Our relationship with the municipality was tense at the beginning – they knew more or less the type of technical support we usually give to other neighbourhoods, related to legalisations and paper work. They started saying: 'Don't think that this neighbourhood will ever be legal' and we answered, 'No, we also think that this plot is not right to build on'. This question of legalisation is also linked to another important fact. It's an agricultural plot; it's really fertile.

We claim for the right to the place but that does not mean to build exactly where it exists. The right to the place, as we see it, is the right of the people to stay nearby, in order to keep their networks, kids to stay in the same school, workers to use the same public transport, etc. We claim for decent houses.

Since we got the funding we began building the kitchen. In fact the space does not function entirely as a kitchen, it's mostly used as a common space. For example, six months after the kitchen opening, the electricity was cut. Everyone was very stressed and organised a general meeting. The pamphlets had the hour and the day, but they forgot to say the location. It was pretty clear to everyone that it was going to take place at the kitchen. It retains its identity. Recently someone started to cook there in order to sell meals for two euros on Saturdays.

We held a lot of meetings with the municipality, and we always tried to help the neighbourhood association. We didn't organise the elections but we participated on the day of the first election in 2014 by participating at the polling stations and counting votes.

This photograph shows the first time the counsellor and the vice-mayor went to the kitchen. It was a very important day. They went there and announced that they would bring tap water there, build a sewage system, and not charge the community for the installation of the water infrastructure or consumption. Almada's municipality has decided that people that prove economic shortcomings will be supplied with five cubic metres of water per month.

Generically speaking we are very focused on designing one process and defining politically the road we want to travel – in distinction to starting from a concept, as we were taught in the university. In this case the political crux was the idea of water. The urgency of water. At the first meeting with the municipality we said that we were not fighting for these people's houses to become legalised because we didn't think the houses were worth being legalised. We are fighting first for the water, which is a human right, and they accepted that as a common ground – that's why it worked.

The municipality, in this case, was not following what the national politicians usually do. For example, public assistance is not allowed in this neighbourhood because most people have no papers, so everything is considered illegal. But the municipality took risks here in regards to the national policies.

The Community Kitchen is illegal, because we don't have a law that can answer to these emergency issues. However we don't want it to become legal, because this will open the door for the neighbourhood to remain in its current precarious conditions.

We received an award for the building, which was really important – not only for us, but also for the people who live there. It has attracted a lot of media

attention. Before starting to talk to the media, we decided on a strategy for the next step. We repeated to everyone that the best prize that the Community Kitchen of Terras da Costa could get was its dismantling, because it would mean that it would not be needed and the neighbourhood would be relocated. This statement was very powerful to deviate the focus from the Kitchen and Prize, to the social conditions people were living in. The prize gave us a way to step forward to do the thing we wanted to do afterwards.

In the meantime, we had no further funding to continue our work there. The visibility given by the prize allowed us to receive a second grant from the Calouste Gulbenkian Foundation. It allowed us to continue the work that we think is relevant, specifically to map and to register the housing, to understand how the houses/people were organised, how inhabitants organised the houses, and so on, in order to design houses according to their needs in the future.

We did a survey of all the houses and started to understand people's seasonal movements, to have updated lists of people that live there, which is very fiuid and changes all the time. This second round of financial support gave us the opportunity to stay in the neighbourhood and to construct a manual of information on the neighbourhood, to get some clues for the new housing process.

We also mapped possible places for residents to be moved, and organised a discussion on where we could build the new neighbourhood with the people. We identified four plots (less then one kilometre away) and we explained our research process to the residents. The idea was not to force them to choose one. We rather wanted to produce material to inform decisions about where and when to build the next neighbourhood. Ultimately, the participatory process results, concerning the plot choice, led to the one we thought was the best. And luckily it was also the one that the municipality was willing to choose.

Flavien Menu Thank you for this presentation. I would like to go back a bit to your trajectory as a firm. You started your office before the crisis, winning competitions and the like, but then you decided to change your attitude and you also decided to stay in Lisbon while your colleagues were leaving for Northern Europe. You have said that you wanted to stay because there was a lot to do but not enough money to do it.

Tiago Mota Saraiva I remember a lecture we gave in Porto in 2007, where we were presented as the most political office of the new Portuguese architects' generation. At least at that time, that wasn't viewed as a positive thing.

When the crisis started, Portuguese Pritzker Prize winners Álvaro Siza and Eduardo Souto de Moura, gave dozens of interviews declaring the failure of

architecture in Portugal, encouraging younger generations to leave the country, saying there was no work to be done over the next few years. Just run for your lives. We answered back by saying: 'No, we look around and there is a lot to be done everywhere. The only thing not working, is that money and energy are not being invested in architecture'. And that's when we started a programme to work with people that need architecture services but have no money to pay for them. We called it: Working with the 99%.

Former energies that we used on architecture competitions, we started to use on designing applications for funding interventions on these neighbourhoods or on designing and building common facilities. If the first experiences were leveraged by us, from one day to another, people started to knock at our door and ask for help. We can build a design programme but also help create informal groups, associations and cooperatives. And, of course, we have now more skills in the team, mostly from social sciences. We changed our way of getting work from one that was focused on winning competitions to one that focuses on fundraising.

During 2016, to best manage this type of project, we decided to also found a co-op: Trabalhar com os 99% [Working with the 99%]. The co-op opens new doors to the practice, establishing it also as an institution to be listened to on new laws and legislations, and that may integrate other NGOs, unions, and neighbourhood associations as members. This urges them to participate on co-op decisions but also provides VAT benefits when using the co-op services.

Joachim Declerck These shantytowns are something that we have seen over the past twenty years as something that is an interesting field for architecture but also for human rights, and the aestheticisation of those rights is clearly taking over. You go beyond the level of saying that there is a temporary installation that is necessary: you define a question, you help draw the first space that enables a community to organise itself, but you also use your expertise to say that it's not permanent. You're quite tough on the same community that you're trying to help. Drawing this process line further than the first installation is something that is exemplary.

We often make a temporary intervention, we often celebrate how fantastic the party is, we often take the photograph, as you did, in the temporary intervention that distinguishes itself from the shantytown and then we stop the arrow of attention: the attention span of the architect is over. I'm interested in the way you work with communities in terms of organising themselves and the way you work with space to help organise this community: it is in these interactions between how cooperatives organise themselves, communities organise themselves,

When the crisis started, Portuguese Pritzker Prize winners Álvaro Siza and Eduardo Souto de Moura gave dozens of interviews declaring the failure of architecture in Portugal, encouraging younger generations to leave the country. We looked around and there was a lot to be done everywhere. So we changed the way we practise to tackle city and people issues in a context of austerity.

and how space can help facilitate this. There is a lot to be won in the area between the organising of communities and the organising of space – there's a lot of work where you can actually reinvent a lot of the conditions of how things could work.

Jeremy Till I have a question that has to do with everyone at the table. Everyone here has been through an architectural education. And architecture education is pretty rubbish generally, it goes down an incredibly conventional set of trajectories, values, aspirations. It might look different but actually it's pretty much the same around the world. Most of you have come out of that and entered into a slightly parallel universe, in which you've taken your skills and your aspirations and have shifted them into a different realm. I'm really interested in what you think is transferable from the conventional norms of architecture values to these other set of rules. And what skills did you bring from the conventional architecture education arena: what do you bring to the table that is different from someone coming from a planning degree or an economics degree? What's your special characteristics?

Tiago Mota Saraiva In Portugal we still have this myth of the architect as a builder, so we were considered false architects – 'architects pretending to be sociologists' as defined by Francisco Aires Mateus after our work being published in *Domus*. But what I really do think is that we are in the process of extending the boundaries of architecture – which is not a new thing. It is not something that is going to destroy other ways of doing it, but it's something that, with the skills of our discipline, we may also do. We have the skills and tools: design abilities, technical know-how, communication skills, paperwork management...

For example, when we started working on the kitchen project, we told the community that we were going to meet with the municipality in order to move forward. For them, the municipality was not different from the police. The police were seen as the aggressors, who were violently trying to displace them and to destroy their livelihoods. But it was important for us to understand that we were going to go through the project procedures as we do with all other projects. So the first thing we did was to go to the municipality and ask about their plans for the territory and the possibility of designing a community kitchen for the neighbourhood.

That's where we assume our architect's profile, or at least, what the society sees and expects of an architect. By the way, usually when I show this project to a conventional audience of architects in Portugal, I always dress myself as a

In Portugal we still have this myth of the architect as a builder.

We were considered false architects – 'architects pretending to be sociologists' as defined by Francisco Aires Mateus after our work being published in *Domus*.

But what I really do think is that we are in the process of extending the boundaries of architecture.

standard architect (mostly in black). It's a matter of representation. Not a representation of the office, but the representation of the excluded neighbourhood.

On the other hand, in the neighbourhoods, it's important to take off this social and dressing barrier, so that people may feel comfortable to complain and criticise. Which they do, a lot. Our experiences are not the experiences of consensus in these participatory processes or in these events; it's an experience of conflict and democracy methods implementation. This has a lot to do with designing the process.

Joachim Declerck There is a world famous sociologist in Brussels who was very critical of architects and their hubris of trying to be involved with everything. He has been critical nearly his entire career, until about two years ago. He recently told me that he shifted his opinion, that he discovered that the incredible force of architect-designers is the project-based mentality of working – that processes always lead to material reality. Architects analyse what the question is, dismantle it, visualise it, check it with others, draw conclusions, maybe draw options so as to help others to decide. The process in government terms – not in all governments – can be endless, that's the typical thing with governmental decision-making processes. He noted that the most design-driven processes always have an ambition to end, preferably not in ten years but in a visible time. In that sense, the magazine is a project for me, an exhibition is a project, and this project mentality is unique to architects and the tools that it gives to others is the unique asset.

Jack Self I was going to say the same thing in a slightly different way: a lot of people are now working on project bases; basically architecture is a mentality, it's a design methodology, and it's a framework or lens for viewing the material world and for tracing the relationship between immaterial processes and material artefact. Increasingly people do not work for a company for their entire lives, they don't work for fifty years in one factory and then get a gold watch. They now work many careers but they work on projects for defined periods of time with fixed outcomes.

And a lot of young people are really struggling because they do not understand the methodology of how projects operate, but they are being forced to work on a project-by-project basis. I think what architects understand, and of course Mies said it very well, is that you don't invent a new architecture every Monday morning. How do you continue your ideas and beliefs if you have a different client, a different site, a different activity, and a different programme for every project? How can you create continuity when every single project demands that you start from scratch? There is both the project in terms of the individual project but also the project of the career, of the life of the architect or of the company.

Our experiences are not the experiences of consensus in these participatory processes or in these events.

It's an experience of conflict and democracy methods implementation.

Jeremy Till It's more than just a project, it's a spatial project in a broader sense of the term – one that goes beyond the formal and engages with the social. That comes from the sensibility and ability to make spatial judgements; it's something we really bring to the table but clearly not in the formal sense.

Joachim Declerk I don't completely agree. You can't consider designing policies as a project. And that's exactly what we need.

Kathryn Firth I wanted to raise something which I didn't learn in school but I feel is a skill that one needs, which is that the architect has to be a mediator – something, as you said, that isn't easy. What are the mechanisms for working when there are voices that are louder than other voices? Is there a kind of holding back that you feel the responsible architect has to do, because you of course have an opinion and you are here as an expert but you don't want to dominate? What are your experiences in that and how do you deal with those situations?

Tiago Mota Saraiva When we presented the four potential plots for the new neighbourhood we were quite clear that we didn't have a previous opinion. We didn't choose what in our technical opinion was the best site. We told the residents that they were going to make a collective decision, and we would also have a technical opinion, afterwards. We were trying to inform the municipality's decision, which had to ultimately purchase the new site's land.

During the presentation of the four potential sites, the president of the neighbourhood association was the only one who was against the idea of relocation. Even his wife and kids were in favour! Of course this produced confiict at a certain point. There is always information that we could not get or understand because we don't live there. You also have to consider that there is a high tax of functional illiteracy and 45 per cent of the people are under eighteen years old. So there are always misunderstandings and irrational moments.

We were not interested in choosing a site for them, but instead we sought to offer choices. We are building spaces of emancipation and if there is too much reluctance we are not going to force anyone. We want the people to be part of the energy we are trying to create. We have no hidden agenda or financial speculative desires.

On top of it, there were still people, in the field, working on a charity basis and giving strength to the idea that they should resist on the plot. This added another layer of complexity. The neoliberal idea that, with some improvements, people 'like them' would live well there. At one point I remember saying in one meeting: 'Our fight is to build new houses with proper conditions. If you agree,

It's more than just a project, it's a spatial project in a broader sense of the term – one that goes beyond the formal and engages with the social.

that's fine, we can continue to fight on your side. If you disagree, that is also fine, but we will step back'.

Flavien Menu Who has the right or power to commission a project? That is, who, how and when can we invent our own brief instead of answering a programme, because even if you try to disrupt it, it will still be commissioned by someone else?

Tiago Mota Saraiva We never asked the municipality if we could work for them. In the beginning we fundraised for the project because we understood that we should keep our independence. But, of course, if we want to build public housing with the municipality and the community, then that would have to be a totally different way of working and funding.

Jack Self OMA-AMO was one of the only models of previous generations that I could see when I was starting REAL. They created the possibility of self-initiating projects from within the studio in what appeared initially to be a quite interesting and independent way. The more I studied that model the more I realised that AMO is just a brand tool. It's not a separate entity. Rem Koolhaas and his team have been setting the direction for their projects for the last thirty years. They say, 'The next thing is the countryside' and they only do projects in the countryside. 'The next thing is China' – and the first building they design in China is CCTV. It's a very successful tool for pursuing what they want to do. They had previously done ten years of research at Harvard in which they used the academy as a lever in order to make lots of connections, so then their first project could be CCTV. REAL, on the other hand, is structured in such a way that in principle goes against the AMO branding relationship to OMA; rather we exist as a cultural foundation which is in fact an architectural firm and therefore we don't have clients in the same way. We can always initiate projects.

Flavien Menu What is important to understand is the lever mechanism for self-initiating projects: what kinds of powers can we trigger? There is also a question of scale here. We are mainly speaking about small-scale projects, but what if we try to self-initiate a large-scale proposal?

Oliver Wainwright I want to bring in a totally different scale of self-initiated projects, which is probably Europe's most expensive, most delayed building: the Elbphilharmonie in Hamburg. Initially it was funded in part by the money of

What is important to understand is the lever mechanism for self-initiating projects: what kinds of powers can we trigger?

There is also a question of scale here. We are mainly speaking about small-scale projects, but what if we try to self-initiate a large-scale proposal?

Jacques Herzog's former classmate, who was a very small time developer in Hamburg. They came up with this incredible vision, self-generated low publicity with this one rendering, and before they knew it the whole state was behind them. So it began as a very small-scale, kind of lucky commercial developer project and his architect mate, and suddenly became Germany's biggest, most expensive, most delayed, arguably most amazing building. Projects can be scalable.

Pooja Agrawal Your mate has to be a commercial developer (*Laughs*).

Oliver Wainwright But he didn't end up developing it. He didn't have the means to develop it. They just made a very convincing image and then the state and the people got behind it and it became a public project because there was such momentum. This is a lesson in the power of publicity, of image making, of taking up a budget without the financial means to build it.

Jack Self We can use our forces as architects for good or evil. What you described is basically the role of image seduction that was prevalent before 2008, in which you didn't have to build the building on the site, you just had to create a seductive image and that was enough to initiate the project.

Kathryn Firth Wouldn't it be better if we could just educate the people that we call clients? The idea that we can do everything on every scale and we don't need anyone and we just say we're collaborative just smacks of the old powerful guard of architects. I much prefer a model where we actually educate people, learn from people who are in the public sector, who are interested in how development happens, and that we actually collaborate with them. I know we're far from that perfect world right now but I think it might be a more sustainable model.

Jack Self I think we already have that situation. You must collaborate with everyone, and to make architecture with the 99 per cent you must also engage productively with the 1 per cent. How do you want to create systemic change if you decide that you are not going to talk to some people? You need to find a way to positively engage with forces that seem opposed or hostile.

Peter Swinnen To wrap up Jeremy's question, I think it's actually quite simple. The task of an architect is to detect clients who don't know yet that they are clients. This could be at a very small scale, as most of the projects we have seen so far. But it can also happen on a big scale. Detecting clients who don't know yet that they are clients is actually how I've experienced my education, how I

You must collaborate with everyone, and to make architecture with the 99 per cent you must also engage productively with the 1 per cent.

How do you want to create systemic change if you decide that you are not going to talk to some people?

You need to find a way to positively engage with forces that seem opposed or hostile.

experienced my first working experience, and that's how I continue to work: in private practice and equally when I was a state architect. Especially in the public sector, to detect clients, political clients is a fantastic thing.

The task of an architect is to detect clients who don't know yet that they are clients.

Detecting clients is actually how I've experienced my education, how I experienced my first working experience, and that's how I continue to work: in private practice and equally when I was a state architect. Especially in the public sector, to detect clients, political clients is a fantastic thing.

Markus Bader, raumlabor

Fountain House, Montreal

Markus Bader, raumlabor I would like to show a photo of some people in raumlabor, just to make clear that I'm not working alone, neither in the office nor on other projects. Somebody discovered we were fifteen years old and so they wrote an article on us and brought a photographer. There are just the people that were there on that particular day. Part of the practice is that we're involved in various projects, very project-based in various cities, so we're rarely ever together in one place.

The picture featured our 'Bye-bye utopia' slogan. It was set up for an exhibition that we did once in KUB Arena in Bregenz and then became our pitchline. It is addressing a sort of dilemma that we feel between the heritage of an architectural utopian project in the background of our architectural education and the actual difficulty in putting a utopian spirit/aspiration into a practice that is implemented in reality.

The project I am going to present refiects this paradox and the way we approach architecture. It is called the Fountain House, which took place in Montreal in 2014. For setting up the project, I spent a lot of time in Montreal, being there and trying to find a sense of this city. Four things struck me during my visit and exploration.

First, being in Montreal as a visitor I discovered a landscape full of these Le Corbusier-type buildings. I walked around and was looking for whatever raised my interest and I discovered Moshe Safdie's Habitat 67, built for the 1967 World's Fair. That was a time when architecture was implemented to create a certain pride in the sense that, 'What we create, projects a future through an object'.

Second example is Buckminster Fuller's American pavilion for the 1967 exposition. Back then hoisting rockets, fiags and everything from the moon age that was supposed to bring us into the future with this Cedric Price idea of technology having the answers, we just need to ask the right question. Now it's a centre for environmental questions, the skin burnt some years ago and it's a sort of remaining dream underpinning the utopian ideal that we can create the future through architecture.

Third, I started to be interested by a series of protests that happened in public spaces in 2012 called the Casseroles movement. The government decided to raise the student fees. In a strong French tradition a sort of revolutionary protest emerged and basically it is a technique of protesting not by carrying banners and making big pamphlets and claims, but by making as much noise as possible with casseroles ie, saucepans. This is also a possibility for everyone to express their solidarity over the common question of the governmental regime of exclusion. This is not accepted through wide areas of society and these protests are proof of such political belief. For me this was an extremely touching use of public space, as a political space primarily, but also as a space where encounter happens.

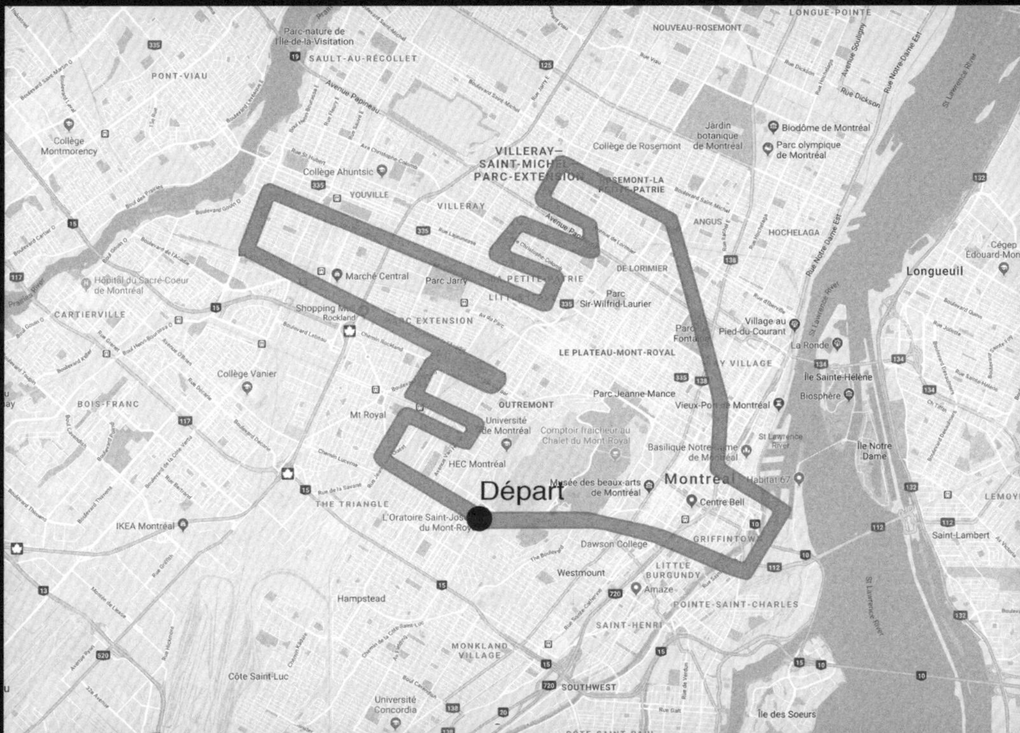
Départ
LONGUE-POINTE
NOUVEAU-ROSEMONT
Parc-nature de l'Île-de-la-Visitation
SAULT-AU-RÉCOLLET
PONT-VIAU
Avenue Papineau
Collège Montmorency
Jardin botanique de Montréal
Biodôme de Montréal
Parc olympique de Montréal
Collège de Rosemont
VILLERAY–SAINT-MICHEL–PARC-EXTENSION
Collège Ahuntsic
YOUVILLE
VILLERAY
ROSEMONT-LA PETITE-PATRIE
ANGUS
HOCHELAGA
Cégep Édouard-Montpetit
Longueuil
Hôpital du Sacré-Coeur de Montréal
Marché Central
Parc Jarry
DE LORIMIER
Parc Sir-Wilfrid-Laurier
CARTIERVILLE
Shopping Mall Rockland
PARC EXTENSION
Village au Pied-du-Courant
La Ronde
LE PLATEAU-MONT-ROYAL
Collège Vanier
Île Sainte-Hélène
Biosphère
BOIS-FRANC
OUTREMONT
Parc Jeanne-Mance
Vieux-Port de Montréal
Mt Royal
Université de Montréal
Comptoir fraîcheur au Chalet du Mont Royal
Basilique Notre-Dame de Montréal
Île Notre Dame
HEC Montréal
Montréal
Habitat 67
Musée des beaux-arts de Montréal
Centre Bell
LEMOYNE
THE TRIANGLE
L'Oratoire Saint-Joseph du Mont-Royal
GRIFFINTOWN
IKEA Montréal
Dawson College
Saint-Lambert
Westmount
LITTLE BURGUNDY
Amaze
Hampstead
POINTE-SAINT-CHARLES
SAINT-HENRI
MONKLAND VILLAGE
Côte Saint-Luc
SOUTHWEST
Université Concordia
Île des Soeurs
CÔTE-SAINT-PAUL

The map on the screen was handed in by the students to the authorities to represent the plan, the trajectory of their protest walk, happening in 2012.

The political struggle was concerned with the Government Issue: the law that tries to limit the right to assemble, to meet in the streets and even the lawyers, as you see in the picture, came out and said 'We don't want to implement that law through our profession'. It was extremely impressive for our practice because we define public space as something that we co-produce; it is not something that just has a status, that is just a given, but something that we create. And this dramatic political example is a dramatic illustration for that.

Fourth, the water – the Saint Lawrence River. It is an amazing force of nature, of resource, of material, of power. It's super impressive; it just permanently runs through the city and I was drowned within its energy. Which led to the question: how does water reach us as a resource?

I thought of water as an invisible service. Looking into the question, I went to the water plant, which is one of three in the city. The plant has this ex-Futurist headquarters with a power room and a control room. I met the lady who is the head of it all. She happily showed me how to clean filters and so on. There are thirty-five people working there, in this amazing piece of architecture. This is highly invisible to a wider public. To a certain extent the architecture represents a pride in the sense of 'we are achieving something for the future' – so it still exists in this mode of 1970s projects.

The infrastructure of the Saint Lawrence can easily take a loss of more than 50 per cent in older pipe systems and they are still operating at only 50 per cent of their capacity. So there is a lot to be said about water management and specific industries in Montreal and the policies around that. There was a political decision in Montreal to provide free water to everyone in the city, directly into their houses, which is really remarkable from a German perspective. When there was a public discussion about taxing the water, the idea was rejected with the argument that the 1 per cent could still fill their pools, because they could easily afford to chip in a bit more money, while for the poorer part of society it would create much more pressure.

These four findings gave birth to the project and we were interested in an intervention re-addressing the idea of public service, and to find a special way to translate this into the urban sphere and the public space.

The programme of Fountain House was very simple: it was a place around a permanently running water tap. I grew up with this paradigm that you have to save; you have to permanently save and you have to be very critical about the resources that you use. This idea of self-limitation is very strongly built into my set of values, which I was both given and have adopted. That value is very

much part of our culture and it is connected to this idea of crisis. In reaction to crisis we pull out these protocols and say, 'Okay, now it's the crisis so we can do the same work with less people, or with less money, and we can impress everyone with the fact that it works even better'. We are coded like that. We need to look at that approach very critically, especially in a city where a resource like water is available in such abundance – which is not true in every space, but this particular city definitely has enough water. Why not just keep the water tap running?

I was looking for a place where the water tap could run permanently, where the water would be permanently available for everyone in the centre of the city. With this programmatic proposal I approached the Goethe Institute and they created links to other institutions in the city like La Biennale de Montreal and the Quartier des Spectacles, which is an interesting new construction, similar to a shopping mall. I chose an empty lot, which is just off Rue Sainte Catherine and on the boundary between Quartier des Spectacles, which is a district undergoing a lot of new development, and the older Montreal, which is known for strip clubs, sex shops and music venues.

In section you can see that there is a possibility to access the roof and enjoy the view. I wanted the outer skin to create something that's changing, that doesn't look like a fortress tower but one that is meant to transmit some kind of idea that this building is alive. This was done very literally by putting earth in between wood and some fabric and letting it grow.

There were a lot of negotiations around allowing it to be an open space, which were driven by a paradigm that we are all familiar with: the paradigm of distress and fear. Montreal has a very strong graffiti scene and people were sure that they would probably leave me two days with this beautiful inner panorama and then it would be covered with graffiti. There was an area nearby that was known as a place where crack users hung, as well as a place that was giving out food and subsidies to homeless people. Through the whole project there were a lot of people saying, 'We need fences, we need to fortify'. These sentiments brought scepticism, they fed the fear of an intervention by these groups while the threat wasn't even there. I hope that my power as an architect and designer of the space is the capacity to produce atmosphere. I try to load space with friendliness, with generosity, with something unexpected.

We designed it so that there was not only water falling down but it collected into this little basin and every now and then in random moments a cloud would appear and bring the building right onto your skin and you could feel it, it enwrapped you. A lot of people came in, just walking by, and used their mobile phones to take a picture – they realised that there was a special moment

mushroom
plant
water
fountain
workshop
cinema
poutine
cooking

happening. That was a very exciting moment for me because I have all these ideas about how it could work and then it happens. Here you see various people doing various things, and the man on the left is somehow embracing the sun coming in. I am interested in whether it's possible to place something that doesn't have a perceivable programme. What happens when we don't have a protocol of how to act – 'this is a public toilet, this is a cinema, this is a car park' or 'this place is associated with specific programmes'?

We worked with a group of artists to engage in a dialogue. The artist Chris Salter engaged in a dialogue about 'what it could be?' or 'how else you might relate to this question of water in the city?' He took the space on as image, for him it was a clock tower, and he put the most powerful strobe and disco folk that he could find to turn it into a dramatic otherness every now and then. The artist Chantal Dumas interviewed people and recorded sounds around the topic of water in and around Montreal. There were various projections by Ælab (Gisèle Trudel) and other artists in Montreal that were working on water-related issues.

Also, the workshop is part of our on-going practice and we build things together, so we built furniture for the public space around. We also organise dinners and collective cooking because that is a powerful way to bring people together.

We try as much as possible to bring these kinds of conversational moments out into the public sphere so that people, while we're discussing public place, can just walk by and listen in. If we want to talk about how to reach people, this is definitely not reaching an everybody audience, but at least it creates visibility for a group of people that are interested in this type of practice and people can slide in and out.

I would like to close with a question. For me this project was an attempt to investigate the question, can work on reversing the narrative of 'we have to cut back, and cut back, and cut back' and readdress or revalue the infrastructures that we have, to find new ways to express ourselves? While all this public money and private money is being spent, can we find moments, critical moments, where we feel that something has a fantastic power that we can also turn to a common or a public benefit?

Pooja Agrawal Who maintains it? Who manages it?

Markus Bader Like most of our projects, this is temporary, so now it's gone. And while it was there, it didn't have a lot of maintenance, just somebody checking in on it every now and then. But of course the management of this kind of project is an issue.

Oliver Wainwright Was there any legacy or afterlife for the project and for that space, for how people conceived that bit of the city?

Flavien Menu I would add something to this question of legacy, you've been practising through these types of interventions for a long time now – 15 years. Perhaps you can give us some insight into your experiences and the legacies of all these temporary pavilions and temporary interventions that you did over that time.

Markus Bader I acknowledge the critic who says that by staying temporary, there might be a certain weakness involved. That all the efforts mentioned before are done, all these people are activated, all these fantasies are being raised and then, the actual material outcome disappears. But the temporary also has a lot of freedom and a lot of opportunity. You can see that as prototyping or creating a sort of imaginary, that you can walk in and even before we all agree that 'all cities need to invest in Fountain Houses' – it's probably good to check if it works.

Flavien Menu Temporary projects often mean low budgets and it underpinsthe question of long-term sustainability of such practices. Temporary projects are great opportunities for young practices to build their first intervention. However, over time there is a need to become more stable and sustainable by building things that are more tangible. All the works we saw today are still really fragile and low-budget, but how to keep that attitude while dealing with larger projects?

Holly Lewis I have to disagree actually. I understand that we're working in different contexts where there are differences in funding structures, but I run a business that employs seventeen people. It pays seventeen rents and seventeen mortgages and that's a proper sized business in the architectural world. And we are doing proper sized projects, they are important, they are not little fiimsy things and we cannot characterise that as fragile. This is exactly what I was talking about: we say, 'It's marginal, it's small, and it's temporary' and we minimise significance and what we're actually doing is dealing with the urban context and making proposals that are appropriate to that context and the outcome. And the fact that it is temporary or small might be right for that time and then I can look at different contexts and use the same tools and analysis and synthesis and propose something that is equally appropriate to a huge scale of redevelopment. So I'm not going to say that we are small or marginal, sorry no.

Temporary projects often mean low budgets and it underpins the question of long-term sustainability of such practices.

Temporary projects are great opportunities for young practices to build their first intervention.

But how to keep that attitude while dealing with larger projects?

Anthony Engi Meacock I think there's a real danger in assuming that big businesses are somehow stable and sustainable – look at the billions corporate companies have lost this year alone.

I think it is strange to say that architects and designers are charitable. It's not embarrassing to make money. We should be proud of being able to make money and also to be able to do what you believe in in that process. Big businesses aren't necessarily more stable or more successful.

This state of mind was challenged a lot in the last financial crash when many major corporate firms went bankrupt. Big firms aren't necessarily stable because they often have corporate structures; we need to get over the feeling that big is stable and sustainable. There are other ways of being financially sustainable and economically viable.

Alex Axinte I have one thought from the margins of Europe. We are close to the Balkans, in the south of Romania. When we go to bed every night we wonder if something has changed. Change is not sudden. Recalling how we began, we were called artists or agitators or all the bad words in the cultural context of Bucharest. But after a while we also started to engage another growth model. It's not that our organisation should grow. We are trained as architects that growing is the goal – you demolish something to replace it with something bigger. We have this DNA of growth. This is true in terms of office organisation as well as an outlook towards society.

One of the most interesting parts of education was unlearning school. It was fun and very creative – it was an opportunity given to us because school was so boring that we had to have this unlearning process. In Bucharest's context, we are working in increasing the alliances, not really the organisation. We are growing our skills. For us, temporary interventions were a way to learn new skills, to test new processes and to bring our knowledge and vision into the public space. We shouldn't make benches out of stone to get successful public spaces. We made a temporary installation seven years ago that is still illegal, but that is producing public space around it. Is it temporary? We are all temporary. How much should we talk about temporariness? I think we should go beyond that. It is more about what uses these temporary installations are constructing, and what spaces are being constructed.

Recently we began to work with civic groups. We have to frame the context: ten years ago in Bucharest there were no civic groups, the notion did not exist, and now there are more than twenty groups. We are collaborating with one of those groups and we are building a community centre together with them, which just opened one month ago. So we are moving forward, not at a large scale but

It is strange to say that architects and designers are charitable. It’s not embarrassing to make money.

We should be proud of being able to make money and also to be able to do what you believe in in that process.

Big businesses aren’t necessarily more stable or more successful.

we are increasing skills within the processes that we are developing. And now we are finally called architects – the scene is calling us architects because there's this recognition of the transformation that these projects are making. I think the potential epidemic of these practices is the most important thing. So, these kind of table discussions, even if they are tiring and in the loop – I've been to this lecture before – I think that they are very good propaganda, if we still want to learn new languages, we have to preach this kind of approach to architectural education. So we have to keep repeating the same lectures.

Jeremy Till One of my favourite quotes is from Brian Eno, who said, 'There are many futures and only one status quo. This is why conservatives mostly agree and radicals always argue.' In a room like this, there is a temptation to never agree. I am worried that there's a group of people that have moved around conferences in the last ten years, and reconvened, and looked at each other, and went away in rooms and have been critical of one another. And I wonder whether we can continue to do that.

I think that there has been a generosity today, which I think should be continued, and I think that there's a need for more collaboration. Because there is a danger that the radicals will continue to disagree. And at this political moment, the radicals need to get together, to fill some gaps.

I have been in a room like this for the last ten years; from Sheffield to Berlin, from Paris to London. And I did something that made people in those rooms very uncomfortable, when I said, 'Actually all we are doing is designing lots of red sheds', because a lot of the architecture coming out of these conventions was basically a kind of garden shed, many painted red. I'm interested in how we move beyond just talking to each other and red sheds, and how we collect another set of people around the table, to have a conversation that is not just an echo chamber or a space of congeniality, but actually engaging productively with people in power as well.

Holly Lewis I think the last thing that we need is more architects staying around and talking to architects. Actually we're already doing these kinds of projects. For the Greater London Authority [GLA], for example, we are engaging with policy-level decision making and research and projects and we should be confident in our work and not say that they're red sheds. We should be ambitious about what we are doing and say, 'I can be at that table because what I have is just as valid as somebody who did some years of law school'. There's a little bit of apologetic behaviour because the architect has this image of being an old man with a stick up his ass and we are not that anymore and

One of my favourite quotes is from Brian Eno, who said, ‘There are many futures and only one status quo. This is why conservatives mostly agree and radicals always argue.’ In a room like this, there is a temptation to never agree.

we need to show that we're not that anymore and I think we need to be more vocal about that.

I don't think we need to all hold hands together and say 'We are a collective, we are a movement', but I think we can have confidence in our projects and say 'The fact that I did that small thing means that I can do a bigger more important thing. And I'll do it well because I do a good job'. I think there's a bit of reticence to stick our heads above the parapet.

Georges are working with the housing ministry in France, shaping policy at the national level – that's incredible! They are a young practice, and they're doing it; historically that wouldn't have been such a problem, just think of all of the incredibly ambitious social housing projects built in Camden. We are not ambitious enough as architects. We resist saying, 'I'm an architect and I can do that'. We should!

Jack Self There is a value to sitting at the table with people that agree with you and doing it consistently for ten years, which sounds funny. To me the value is – and it's the same reason that I write – everyone thinks they know what they believe, and everyone thinks they know what they think. But the act of saying something out loud is powerful. This is the first time I presented *Real Review*, and I'm not going to present it that way again – because only when I said things out loud, did I realise that a lot of stuff didn't make a lot of sense. The opportunity to do it again in the future will change my ideas as well, so I think there is real value in being able to discuss and debate with other people, clarifying our own positions and our own opinions, and being forced to present them to other people as well.

Tiago Mota Saraiva We have to be aware that organising collective discussion could have a powerful effect. For example, in Spain, dozens and dozens of architectural collectives have emerged in the last decade and a lot were engaged in the campaigns for electing Manuela Carmena (Madrid) or Ada Colau (Barcelona).

They brought together their knowledge and forces to produce content and solutions for the cities. For instance, they organised discussions with citizens in fragile areas to understand their needs. During the campaign they helped with methodologies that emerged from their daily work as collectives – tools sometimes, used for temporary interventions. They were brought to another level when used for political strength.

We use the same strategy in our work. Being close to people's aims, gives us the knowledge. We constantly need to speak to others for building up our

We have to be aware that organising collective discussion could have a powerful effect.

In Spain, dozens and dozens of architectural collectives have emerged in the last decade and a lot were engaged in the campaigns for electing Manuela Carmena (Madrid) or Ada Colau (Barcelona).

political infiuence. At the moment we are often called for solving problems that are not only architectural, at first glance. We have housing projects for the Romany community, for example. Our projects do not start with a sketch but through talking to people, stakeholders and other architects to understand problems, needs and alternatives. Our daily life is filled with trying to tackle prejudice and racism for instance, and you have to collectively discuss to open people's eyes and minds.

It is a matter of battles that you decide to dispute and I am really convinced that speaking to each other, criticising and debating is the way to strengthen the power of our processes. Our Terras da Costa project would never have been like that without the help of Exyzt/Constructlab, for example, who provided the wood for the Community Kitchen construction.

Right now I feel that we are in a symbiotic spirit between practices for building up common good, rather than the classic competitive practice of fighting between each other for commissions and individual reputation.

Flavien Menu The idea of creating common good often underpinned public sector management. This idea – or maybe this lure – has been evocated a lot today while we often opposed public sector as good and private sector as evil, but it could also sound like a rhetorical tool for right-thinking indignation.

Oliver Wainwright There is the answer that the public sector pays a lot better than the private sector at the moment. If you are a practice looking to grow in the United Kingdom, you know that with developers the architect's fee gets relentlessly squeezed down more so than in the public sector, which has, over the past five years, spent a lot on regeneration and housing. It's counterintuitive to what is generally agreed upon, but it's the way to make a profitable start-up today.

Holly Lewis Whenever we've been approached by private developers, we don't share a motivation for why we're delivering the project. Our motivation is that we do the best possible project and their motivation is financial. And I don't want to tar all developers with the same brush and I'm sure that there are some that don't feel like that, but we have never been approached by one who shares our full vision. And we're busy enough with the public sector, so I don't feel that we need to have this massive expansion plan into the private sector. But I don't deny that there's private money in what we're delivering – Section 106 is funded by the state's income from delivering private development and we are shaping private development, so by doing some kind of planning documents or masterplan we are shaping private development.

The idea of creating common good often underpinned public sector management.

This idea – or maybe this lure – has been evocated a lot today while we often opposed public sector as good and private sector as evil, but it could also sound like a rhetorical tool for right-thinking indignation.

So we are not disengaged from the private sector. But if they have given their money to a local authority I prefer to work with the local authority, just in terms of motivation for how to deliver the project. But absolutely, our practice is run because the private sector is spending its money. In all of our projects we are never spending central government money, we are spending developers' money but we do it through different channels that we find to be more ethically comfortable.

Flavien Menu Oliver, you said that using public money is the best way to start your practice, but then when you want to grow, what do you do? You have to deal with the private money, right?

Oliver Wainwright Section 106 is a planning gain; every time there is a private development of a certain type of proportion, the local council can go in and cream off the top of that. It's a mitigating impact of private development that has to be spent on improving public roads, parks, plantings, primary schools ... I think there is an entire branch of practice that only works with Section 106 budgets. The percentage funding for art programmes is similar to Section 106 and that could be cleverly diverted toward things, which aren't conventional public art, there's an avenue for smaller practices to exploit.

Jack Self We try to bite off more than we can chew. This is not my point actually, it's Mark Cousins': architecture is an intrinsically failed profession in terms of our inability to monopolise the field that we set out to colonise. Before the middle of the nineteenth century there was no professionalisation of doctors or lawyers, anyone could practice, and then there was this thing about quack doctors and suddenly only a doctor with certain qualifications can be a doctor; this was also true with lawyers. And doctors have a monopoly on the treatment of the body, lawyers have a monopoly over the law – architects don't have a monopoly over everything that's built, they can't, so it was a failure in that sense.

Joachim Declerck Come to Belgium! It's the most disorganised part of urbanised Europe, but everything you build has to be drawn by an architect. But it's not a guarantee for more or better pay, or for better urban development.

There are many different discussions going on: one, this practice should not be marginalised and especially not by the practice itself; two, there is the question of pay; three, I think the reason we are also sitting together is because if you listen to some of our stories, many focus on certain challenges we face. The gap between what we are able to do now as fantastic experiments and the things we

Architecture is an intrinsically failed profession in terms of our inability to monopolise the field that we set out to colonise.

should be able to do is big. Part of the challenge we have is to find ways to close that gap and multiply our strategies for doing so. In that sense, when we say, 'We have a lot to do, and we are marginal', it's not that the practice is marginal as a practice, it's that what we are able to achieve is marginal compared to what we need to achieve.

Anthony Engi Meacock The idea that architects traditionally have been very bad at justifying their value is interesting. The image of the artist-architect-genius who draws a sketch on a napkin is actually very damaging. What is also interesting about lots of people around the table is this engagement with the language of business – engaging with that rhetoric even if you disagree with it. Engaging the private sector doesn't mean actually working for the private sector; you can also change it. If we don't understand, then we can't change and we can't survive.

Mathieu Delorme I would like to add something about language and the private sector: how can we as architects know or learn the language of economics? Because the failure of architects is that they don't know where the money comes from. We need to make a shortcut in order to involve the money that is surrounding us rather than making a financially-motivated trip – going to New York or Shanghai. The language of architects is now increasingly about economy. We all have to go to business school or do a PhD in economics to create our own tools, we need money for architecture and we have to create that.

Jack Self And the point is really to make sure that you understand those financial tools as part of a financial design process, which is also part of architecture. For example, in Britain it's extremely rare to get a mortgage on a property that's more than five storeys above the ground, because it's considered too risky, which means that high-rise typologies are either for extremely wealthy people who can buy it outright or for people who live in 1970s social housing. So an entire typology of the built environment becomes impossible because of the terms and conditions of a mortgage. I'm sure you've met people who work in financial institutions, many of them are very brilliant, many developers are also very brilliant. But the ability to resolve whether or not you can get water to run from a toilet back to a core is way more complicated than designing a mortgage. If architects can absorb financial thinking into our way of working it would give us a new type of agency and power.

What is interesting about lots of people around the table is this engagement with the language of business – engaging with that rhetoric even if you disagree with it.

Engaging the private sector doesn’t mean actually working for the private sector; you can also change it.

If we don’t understand, then we can’t change and we can’t survive.

Return of Investment (SROI)

Biographies

Pooja Agrawal is an architect working on regeneration at the Greater London Authority. Prior to the GLA, she worked as an architect and an urban designer at practices including We Made That and Publica. The common thread running through her career is the ambition to create beautiful places with a public agenda. Pooja is also a member of Design South East – a design review panel for the SE of England, a guest tutor at Central Saint Martins and is a key member of StART, a community land trust campaigning to build 800 affordable homes in Tottenham.

Assemble: Anthony Engi Meacock
Assemble are a collective of 15 whose work addresses the relationship between people and the built environment. Assemble take a hands-on, collaborative approach, and whilst their work usually includes design it rarely starts or ends there, often employing a range of means from the social to the infrastructural to make spaces which enable independence, self-authorship, creativity and difference. Assemble started working together informally in 2009, and delivered their first project, the Cineroleum in 2010. Working in their free-time and around other jobs, they built the Cineroleum from borrowed, recycled and industrial materials, with around 200 friends, volunteers and passers-by. The collective of 15 which was established through this project has retained a non-hierarchical structure and interdisciplinary ethos and now works across the UK, for both independent community groups and public bodies, and on both self-initiated and commissioned projects.

ateliergeorges: Aurélien Delchet & Mathieu Delorme
ateliergeorges, established by two architects and two landscape engineers, is a young office identified for its work both at the urban and territorial scale (French Young Planners Award 2014, winner of Europan sessions 11, 12 and 13) and for its openness to a wider set of stakeholders. The office has developed a working method of 'negotiating place' that puts co-production at the heart of the city's manufacturing process. From Haute-Correze to Shanghai, from design to real estate management – the office was born from the desire to start a conversation with the entire production line of the inhabited environment. Theory and practice are combined at Georges; all the partners have a teaching activity: in the architecture schools of Paris-Belleville, Paris-La Villette and Marne-la-Vallée, but also at the National Ecole des Ponts-et-Chaussées and the National Conservatory of Arts and Crafts.

Aurélien Delchet is a French architect who graduated from ENSA

Clermont-Ferrand. He teaches at ENSAVT Marne-la-Vallée. At the end of school, Aurélien already had a solid experience of the architectural practice. He chose to put his knowledge of the genesis of the project and the form into perspective by expatriating himself, first to Amsterdam, at Claus en Kaan – where he had the opportunity to observe the association of construction with industry rather than craft – and then to London – where the public project interest has already begun to undergo profound changes.

Mathieu Delorme is a landscape engineer from the School of Nature and Landscape (ENP) in Blois (INSA Val-de-Loire Centre) and an urban planner who graduated from ESSEC with a master's degree in Urban Management and Real Estate (MUI). He teaches at ENSAVT in Marne-la-Vallée (ecology and project economics), at the EN of the Ponts-et-Chaussées (eco-design of the city) and at ENP de Blois (strategy of city stakeholders).Mathieu began his professional life with the project management of the prefiguration of the Public Establishment of Paris-Saclay mission. This experience was foundational. In this territory where stakeholder games and the challenges of metropolitan development are the most exacerbated, project practice is not possible without the conception of a real negotiation strategy. It also realises the limits of traditional methods of development and planning in the transformation of a compartmentalised territory into a system dedicated to innovation. Lighter schemes of animation, accompaniment of project developer, citizen or entrepreneurial initiatives, are to be invented.

Ateliermob: Tiago Mota Saraiva
Ateliermob is a multidisciplinary platform for the development of ideas, research and projects in the areas of architecture, design and urbanism. The company was founded in 2005 in Lisbon, as a result of several works carried out by its founding partners. In 2016, Working with the 99% cooperative was created for the provision of services in the fields of architecture and social or intervention design, spatial practices, urban planning, strategic planning, coordination and implementation of projects and training that were already being developed under Ateliermob's scope. At the same time, this platform has been developing research work to support project practice, an online architecture website, architectural design, urban planning and it has maintained a regular presence in various forums and national and international networks such as the European ReKreators network, the observatory of Mexico City started by Unesco, DLBC Lisbon Network,

the laboratory of participatory practices developed in the region of Basilicata, Italy, or the official representation of Portugal at the Venice Architecture Biennale 2014.

Tiago Mota Saraiva is an architect, urbanist and planner. He has a degree in Architecture and a specialisation in Architecture, Territory and Memory. Since 1995 he has worked in several offices in Lisbon, Rome and Vicenza. He was Invited Assistant Professor at Universidade Moderna (2007) and at FAUTL (2007–2008). Tiago is an Effective Member of the Architects Board National Association since 2001, having been part of its National Executive Board (2003–07) and National Treasurer (2005–2007). He was a Member of the Organising Committee of the Portuguese National Architecture Year 2003 and one of the curators for the International Celebration of Cities Competition, organised by the UIA. He was Portuguese delegate in the International Union of Architects Congress of 2005 in Istanbul, Turkey. Currently, he is managing partner at Ateliermob and director of 'Working with the 99%' co-op; he writes a weekly opinion column in *i* (daily national newspaper) and is member of Le Monde Diplomatique – Portuguese Version; he is a board member of the cultural/social co-op Largo Residências and Rekreators European Association; and he is external advisor of Lisbon City Council on the group for the implementation of the Agenda 21 for Culture.

Joachim Declerck is a founder and partner of the Architecture Workroom Brussels. Educated as an architect and urban designer at Ghent University (BE) and the Berlage Institute (NL), Declerck's activities focus on innovation within the disciplines of architecture and urban design, while exploring their role within the transformation of the built environment.

Melanie Dodd is an architect and academic, currently Programme Director of Spatial Practices at Central Saint Martins. Educated at Cambridge, she has taught architecture at a range of institutions since 1995, including London Metropolitan University (CASS), Royal College of Art, and RMIT University in Melbourne, where she was Programme Director of Architecture from 2005–2013. She has been a collaborator with muf architecture/art since 1997. Both her teaching, practice and research interests focus on the relationships between social and political infrastructures, and built environments, explored in her book *Live Projects: Designing with*

People (RMIT Press, 2012) and her PhD By Practice (RMIT 2011).

Kathryn Firth works on masterplanning and urban regeneration projects in the US, Europe, the Middle East and the UK for both the private and public sectors. She is currently focused on large-scale regeneration projects in both the UK and the US. She was the Chief of Design at the London Legacy Development Corporation (LLDC) from 2011–2015 where she was responsible for design direction and implementation of multiple masterplans and guidance for planning applications.

Harriet Harriss is largely focused upon pioneering new pedagogic models for design education in her teaching, research and writing, particularly those models that respond to specific community challenges: as captured in her most recent publications, *Architecture Live Projects: Pedagogy into Practice* (Routledge, 2014); and *Radical Pedagogies: Architecture & the British Tradition* (RIBA Publishing, 2015). Her most recent publication, *A Gendered Profession* (RIBA publishing, 2016) asserts the need for widening participation in architecture, as a means to ensure the profession remains as diverse as the society it seeks to serve.

Flavien Menu is a London–Paris based architect with a postgraduate dual degree in urban policies (Sciences Po Paris/London School of Economics).

Flavien founded Office for Cities, a strategic consultancy office at the crossroads of politics, economics and architecture aiming to facilitate exchanges, building partnerships and to target innovative strategies in accordance with territorial and societal realities. Alongside his practice, Flavien is extensively writing and debating to actively fuel the social, political and cultural debate on built environment issues. Recently, Flavien talked at Harvard Kennedy School University for the European conference. Flavien has taught at the Architectural Association and intervenes in various academic institutions such as Sciences Po Paris, London School of Economics, Royal College of Art, Columbia GSAPP and ETH Zurich.

raumlabor: Markus Bader
raumlabor is a Berlin-based collective of nine practitioners created in 1999. raumlabor works between architecture, urbanism, and artistic practices. raumlabor strongly believe in complexity and that our society today needs a more substantial approach, therefore their spatial proposals are small scale and deeply rooted in the local condition.

Markus Bader is co-founder of raumlabor Berlin, which focuses on urban strategies and procedural urban development, as well as curatorial and spatial installation work on the intersections of art and the city of Berlin. He holds degrees in architecture from the Technical University of Berlin, the Berlin University of the Arts, and the Bartlett School of Architecture in London. Key projects have included creating concepts for activating Tempelhof Airport in Berlin (2007–2009); co-authoring concepts for the international building exhibition Berlin 2020 'City Capital – Spacious City, Instant City' (2010–2011); and artistic direction of 'The KNOT', an experiment on collaborative art in public urban spaces in Berlin, Warsaw, and Bucharest (2010). Previously, Markus has served as a guest professor at Peter Behrens School of Architecture, Düsseldorf and at Academy of Applied Arts (VSUP) Prague; and as assistant professor at Brandenburgische Technische Universität Cottbus.

REAL: Jack Self

REAL is a London-based cultural institute and architectural practice founded by Jack Self in 2016. REAL understands architecture as a spatial practice, and real estate as a manifestation of complex social, political and economic power relations. REAL is focused on how property and ownership, forms of labour, and our management of time affect our everyday lives. REAL is a collaborative organisation, with light bureaucracy and minimal overheads. Wherever possible it seeks to utilise the existing structures of its partners to reduce redundancy, improve productivity, foster inclusivity, and promote collective enquiry. It is above all dedicated to the highest quality of intellectual and creative output. REAL's projects include exhibitions, publishing and architecture. Our partners and clients are cultural and financial institutions, developers, housing associations, private companies, and a broad network of architects, artists and designers.

Jack Self is an architect based in London. He is Director of the REAL foundation and Editor-in-Chief of the *Real Review*. In 2016, Jack curated the British Pavilion at the Venice Architecture Biennale. Jack's architectural design focuses on alternative models of ownership, contemporary forms of labour, and the formation of socio-economic power relationships in space. His work has been shown widely, including at the Maxxi in Rome and the Tate Britain in London. Jack's writing has appeared in *The Guardian*, *eflux*, *New Philosopher*, BBC, CNN and elsewhere. Jack's first book *Real Estates: Life Without Debt* (Bedford Press, 2014) is now in its second printing.

He was previously Contributing Editor for *Architectural Review* (2009–2017) and is Editor-at-Large for *032c*.

studioBASAR: Alex Axinte & Cristi Borcan
studioBASAR is a Bucharest based architectural studio and a public space practice founded in 2006 by Alex Axinte and Cristi Borcan. Preoccupied with the dynamics of urban culture and the disappearing importance of public spaces, studioBASAR initiates and develops actions and projects within public space. Ranging from temporary to permanent, these processes include applied research, community activation, participatory programming, urban design and live education.

Alex is an architect working and living in Bucharest, Romania. He graduated in 2004 from the 'Ion Mincu' University of Architecture and Urbanism in Bucharest. In 2006 he co-founded, together with Cristi Borcan, studioBASAR as an architectural studio and public space practice. He is currently undertaking a MA in Social Sciences, part of a PhD by practice at the University of Sheffield, UK.

Cristi Borcan is a Bucharest based architect and co-founder of studioBASAR. In 2017 studioBASAR was one of the honorees of the Social Design Circle awarded by Curry Stone Design Prize and in 2018 one of the recipients of The National Cultural Fund Award.

Peter Swinnen is a Brussels based architect. He currently practises architecture at CRIT, conducts PhD research on the political praxis of architecture (KUL University) and runs the ETH Zürich design studio on architectural policy whispering.

Jeremy Till is an architect, writer and educator. His research is known for exploring the social and political dimensions of architecture and the built environment. Till's major written work is *Architecture Depends* (2009), which suggests a new way of understanding architecture in terms of its dependency rather than its autonomy.

Oliver Wainwright is *The Guardian*'s architecture and design critic. Trained as an architect, he has worked for a number of practices, both in the UK and overseas, and written extensively on architecture and design for many international publications. He is also a visiting critic at several architecture schools.

We Made That: Holly Lewis
Holly co-founded We Made That in 2006. She has led a unique range of urban projects for the practice, from pioneering industrial intensification

work through to comprehensive high street regeneration projects. This includes the research portfolio of the practice, with particularly incisive studies of local economies and placemaking across London. Holly graduated from the Bartlett School of Architecture; she is a registered architect and affiliate member of the Landscape Institute. She was shortlisted for the AJ Emerging Woman Architect of the Year Award 2012. In her roles as Mayor's Design Advocate for the Greater London Authority and CABE Built Environment Expert, Holly advocates for community involvement within the design process, empowering women in the built environment and equitable city-making.

Holly has taught BSc Architecture at the Bartlett School of Architecture, UCL and London Metropolitan University. She has also lectured in the UK and abroad, including Russia, Denmark, Spain and Argentina. Holly is a trustee of The Architecture Foundation. We Made That is an energetic architecture and urbanism practice with a strong public conscience. Established in 2006, We Made That works with public sector clients to prepare incisive urban research, to develop responsive area strategies and masterplans and to deliver distinctive architecture and public realm projects. All We Made That work is public, and it aims to make imaginative and considered contributions to the built environment through socially engaged design processes. They have worked with a number of public and local authority clients, including recent projects for 22 of London's 33 boroughs; the Greater London Authority, Lee Valley Regional Park Authority, LLDC, Olympic Delivery Authority and Transport for London.

Image Credits

20–21 © Flavien Menu
25, 29 © Jakob Spriestersbach
27, 33 Courtesy We Made That
47, 49, 51 Courtesy ateliergeorges and Bellastock
63, 65, 67, 69, 71 © studioBASAR
6–7, 98–99, 178–179 © Valerie Bennett, Architectural Association
103, 111, 113 Courtesy Assemble
105, 107 Courtesy Assemble and Eleanor Lee
109 Courtesy Assemble and Marie Jacotey
117, 119, 121, 123 Courtesy Jack Self, REAL Foundation and *Real Review*
133, 137, 139 Courtesy Ateliermob
135 Courtesy Fernando Guerra/ FG+SG
157, 159, 161, 163 Courtesy raumlabor

Acknowledgements

Brett Steele
Barbara-Ann Campbell-Lange
Manijeh Verghese
Peter Swinnen
Max Kahlen
Thomas Weaver
Tobias Hentzer Dausgaard
Blandine Rambaud

Frédérique Barchelard

This book would not have been possible without the support of the Architectural Association where the Bedford Tapes events took place on 9 December 2016 and the trust of Brett Steele and Manijeh Verghese who let me organise this seminal event.

This book would never have had such energy without the enthusiasm of its contributors, who have always been available to share their thoughts and expertise.

Colophon

Editing: Flavien Menu
Concept: Flavien Menu and Wayne Daly
Graphic design: Daly & Lyon
Lithography: Hausstætter Herstellung, Berlin
Copyediting: Leah Whitman-Salkin
Proofreading: Clare Barrett
Printing: Druckhaus Köthen

Published by:
Spector Books
Harkortstraße 10
04107 Leipzig
www.spectorbooks.com

Distribution:
Germany, Austria: GVA, Gemeinsame Verlagsauslieferung Göttingen GmbH&Co. KG, www.gva-verlage.de
Switzerland: AVA Verlagsauslieferung AG, www.ava.ch
France, Belgium: Interart Paris, www.interart.fr
UK: Central Books Ltd, www.centralbooks.com
USA, Canada, Central and South America, Africa, Asia: ARTBOOK/D.A.P., www.artbook.com
South Korea: The Book Society, www.thebooksociety.org
Australia, New Zealand: Perimeter Distribution, www.perimeterdistribution.com

First edition: 2018

Printed in Germany

ISBN 978-3-95905-206-1

We need
spaces th
us confid
invent ne
forms

to create
at give
ence to
v public

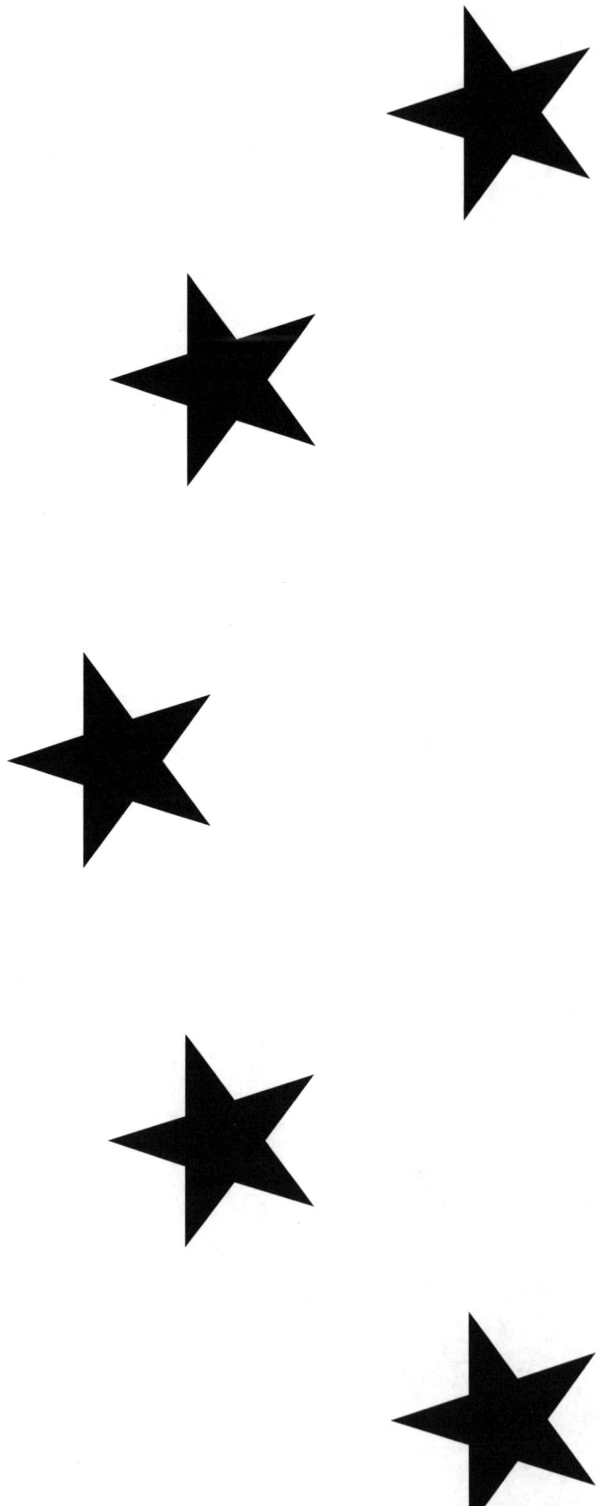